Mountain Biking
Georgia

Alex Nutt

FALCON®

Guilford, Connecticut
An imprint of The Globe Pequot Press

A FALCON GUIDE ®

© 1998 Falcon® Publishing
  Published by The Globe Pequot Press, Guilford, Connecticut

Falcon and FalconGuide are registered trademarks of The Globe Pequot Press.

Cover photo by Robb Helfrick.
Inside black-and-white photos by Anne Ledbetter.

Library of Congress Cataloging-in-Publication Data

Nutt, Alex
    Mountain Biking Georgia / by Alex Nutt
        p.   cm.
    ISBN 1-56044-647-1 (pbk. : alk. paper)
    1. All terrain cycling—Georgia—Guidebooks. 2. Bicycle trails—
Georgia—Guidebooks. 3. Georgia—Guidebooks. I. Title
GV0145.5.G28N88   1998
917.5804'43—dc21   98-40717
                                                        CIP

♻ Text pages printed on recycled paper.

Manufactured in the United States of America
First Edition/Third Printing

CAUTION
Outdoor recreational activities are by their very nature potentially hazardous. All participants in such activities must assume the responsibility for their own actions and safety. The information contained in this guidebook cannot replace sound judgment and good decision-making skills, which help reduce risk exposure, nor does the scope of this book allow for disclosure of all the potential hazards and risks involved in such activities.

Learn as much as possible about the outdoor recreational activities in which you participate, prepare for the unexpected, and be cautious. The reward will be a safer and more enjoyable experience.

Contents

Acknowledgments

This book would not have been possible without the cooperation and assistance of so many people. I hope I haven't missed anyone.

From the USDA Forest Service; Larry Thomas and Mike Davis from the Cohutta District; Tony Rider, Edwin Dale, Milton Bradley, Gordon Riddock, Kent Evans, and Sherry Payne from the Toccoa District; and Robert E. Lee from the Ocoee District.

Wally Woods and Brian Ensley from Fort Mountain State Park, Bill Tinley and Joe Bradford from Mistletoe State Park, William Bentley and Ellen McConnell from Unicoi State Park, and Bill Tanner and David Perry from Tallulah Gorge State Park.

Paul Molla and Allen Dean from the U.S. Army Corps of Engineers.

Burt Weertz, Henry Chambers, and Alicia Soriano from the Georgia Department of Natural Resources.

Woody from SORBA-Helen, Lester Ramey from SORBA-NE Georgia; Frank Ward, Freddie Walker, Sherry Walker, and Mike Palmeri from SORBA-EMBA in Ellijay; Tom Sauret, Belinda Sauret, and Glen Akins from SORBA-Gainesville; and Keith McFadden from SORBA-Atlanta.

Thanks to Bill Victor for showing me that trails do exist in the eastern part of the state. Extra thanks to Steve Houghton for stepping in and helping out when the deadline loomed. Thanks to Jay Franklin for talking me into this to start with, and for being such a dedicated advocate for so many of the trails described herein.

Thanks to David Mayne, who showed me what it really means to be a volunteer.

Special thanks to Mike Maness, who accompanied me on most of these rides and offered much in the way of an entertaining riding style and a lot of attitude adjustments.

To my editors at Falcon, first Randall Green, then John Burbidge (I took so long Randall got bored and went to a project that actually moved). Your patience and guidance are more appreciated than you know. I hope the results justify the wait.

And finally and most importantly, I couldn't have written this book without the patience, blessing, help, and encouragement of my wife, Kim. She spent many hours transcribing barely understandable recordings of me sucking wind while trying to impart some pertinent information. Add to that the normal clatter of a heavily laden bike and graceless rider covering rough trails, and her contributions become even more admirable. Kim had to be both mom and dad on way too many occasions while I was out doing research. My children are young, and should soon forget that Dad was sure gone a lot this past year, and sure sat at the computer a lot whenever he was home. To Stephanie, Trace, and AJ, this ultimately is for you.

Few of the rides in this book would even exist without the ongoing dedication and hard volunteer work of the members of SORBA and its chapters, and all of the other volunteers and groups that contribute time and effort to make so many trails possible. You folks are the real heroes, and I'm constantly amazed at how much a dedicated group of enthusiasts can accomplish. I'm proud to be a part of such a group.

I used a Cateye AT100 cycle altimeter/computer to map these trails. I mention this because I had good luck with a relatively inexpensive product, and I'm happy to mention something that works. The units I used are now well over a year old, with much abuse and wear, and other than changing batteries, I've done no maintenance on them and had no problem with them.

I rode a Cannondale SVA with a Headshock fork for the entire time. The frame was consistently smooth, flex-free, and required no maintenance. With Shimano XTR parts, I changed nothing but chains, cassettes, and derailleur pulleys. You get what you pay for.

WTB tires are very common here and for good reason. They do well in everything but wet autumn leaves—no tires are good in wet autumn leaves. I've had less luck with wheels, however. I finally purchased a set of composite wheels, which cured my wheel woes.

I have not received favors or products from the above mentioned manufacturers (not that I wouldn't happily do so!), but I believe that if a product works, you should tell folks. While writing this book, I had to ride a less-than-perfectly maintained bike on too many occasions, and the only mechanical failure I experienced was a broken chain. If you count my Clydesdale weight and not-too-fluid riding style, the lack of mechanicals seems unlikely.

Map Legend

Interstate		Campground	
U.S. Highway		Picnic Area	
State or Other Principal Road		Buildings	
Forest Road		Peak/Elevation	4,507 ft.
Interstate Highway		Bridge/Pass	
Paved Road		Gate	
Gravel Road		Parking Area	
Unimproved Road		Boardwalk/Pier	
Trail (singletrack)		Railroad Track	
Trailhead		Cliffs/Bluff	
Trail Marker		Power Line	
Waterway		Forest Boundary	
Intermittent Waterway		Map Orientation	N
Lake/Reservoir		Scale	0 0.5 1 MILES
Meadow/Swamp			

Statewide Locator Map

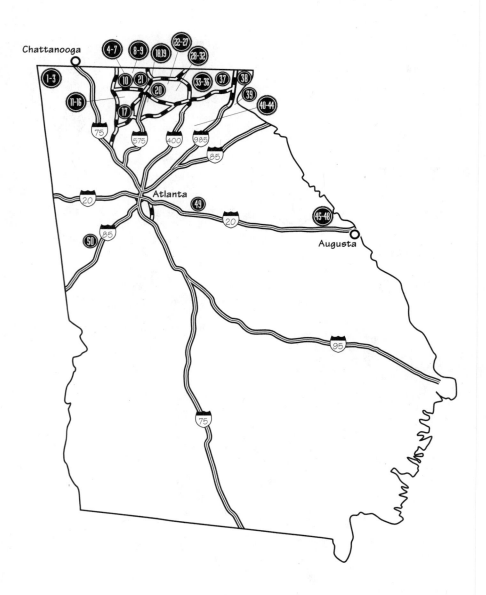

About This Book

There's a lot in print about the trails in Georgia, but that information is widely scattered, not easily located, and often contradictory. It's amazing how remarkably fluid the status of trails can be.

Every effort has been made to ensure the accuracy of the information contained herein. Some of the information may have changed between the time I wrote it and publication. Land access is a dynamic world here and things sometimes change rapidly. I have included telephone numbers in the appendices so that you can get the latest trail status.

I mapped the trails described by riding each trail with an altimeter and cycle computer. I recorded elevation readings every 0.1 mile, and turns or intersections whenever they occurred. I used a second altimeter and cycle computer on most rides for verification and backup.

The elevation graphs are believed to be accurate; however, they are not to scale. The graphs are designed to give an overview of the contours of a ride, not to be taken literally. Atmospheric or temperature changes may affect the readings. I have attempted to check this information against known accurate information such as topographic maps whenever possible. The elevation and mileage readings are for reference only.

Maps were drawn from existing maps, usually supplied by the land manager of the trail in question, and taken from U.S. Geological Survey or Forest Service maps. The maps in this book are intended to be a rough guide, to show the layout and general direction of the trail configuration. As with all of the information contained herein, routes or conditions may change. Use good judgment.

USING THIS GUIDE

The first section of each ride description has an overview of the pertinent information on that trail.

The **name** of the trail and the number as it appears in this guide are listed at the top of the page.

Location refers to the trail's physical location in the state. I used Atlanta as the reference point for all the rides.

Distance refers to the length of the trail or loop as described in this guide.

Time refers to the length of time an average rider would take to ride the trail. The time is based on an average speed for most trails, and does not include stops and breaks. This one is subjective.

Tread refers to the trail surface and makeup. The four types of tread listed are singletrack, doubletrack, gravel roads, and paved roads. The difference between singletrack and doubletrack can be subtle.

Aerobic level refers to the relative physical difficulty of riding the trail.

Technical difficulty refers to the level of bike-handling skill needed to ride the trail.

Highlights are the features that stand out on this particular ride.

Alex Nutt handles a rocky trail.

Land status refers to the ownership and/or management of the land on which the trail is located; also indicates trail as multi-use where applicable.

Maps refers to the USGS 7.5-minute quad map of the area. The trail may not be on the quad map, but the map can give you an idea of the terrain and features.

Access pertains to how to reach the trailhead. Again, directions are given from Atlanta.

AEROBIC LEVEL RATINGS

An **easy** ride is just that—a ride that anyone in reasonable shape with a reasonably serviceable bike can do. Easy rides are usually less than 10 miles long, combined with relatively flat ground and few climbs.

There may be an occasional moderate section in an easy ride. An easy ride is relative to the other levels of difficulty in this book, and is not necessarily a paved bike path. Easy rides are usually rated between 1 and 3 in difficulty.

A **moderate** ride is more difficult than an easy ride, is usually from 5 to 15 miles in length, includes more varied terrain with some extended climbs and descents, and has more technical sections. There may be easy and strenuous sections in a moderate ride. Moderate rides are usually rated between 2 and 4 in difficulty.

A **strenuous** ride is the most difficult. These rides include a combination of distance, terrain, and technical difficulty that will test your fitness and skills. There may be easy or moderate sections in a strenuous ride. Strenuous rides are usually rated between 3 and 5 in difficulty.

TECHNICAL DIFFICULTY RATINGS

The degree of technical skills necessary to safely complete a ride is rated on a scale of 1 to 5, with 1 being the easiest and 5 the most difficult.

A technical difficulty of 1 means that the trail surface is fairly smooth and flat, with no appreciable obstacles.

A technical difficulty of 2 means that the trail is smooth and flat, but may have small hills, log or stream crossings, and other easily negotiated obstacles.

A technical difficulty of 3 means that the trail surface is rough and irregular in some areas. The trail has some extended climbs, descents, and more difficult stream or creek crossings, dips, drop-offs, switchbacks, and narrow sections of singletrack. There may be other obstacles.

A technical difficulty of 4 means the trail surface is even more irregular and varied than a trail with a technical difficulty of 3. The trail has more of the difficult and extended climbs and descents; rocky, deep, and difficult creek crossings; tight switchbacks; and narrow singletrack with drops to one or both sides. There may be other obstacles as well.

A technical difficulty of 5 means that the trail surface is very rough and irregular. The trail has steep and/or extended climbs and descents, very tight switchbacks, deep creek crossings, drop-offs to the side of the trail, numerous rough and obstacle-covered sections that are difficult to negotiate, and steep pitches and drop-offs. There may be other types of obstacles.

These ratings are subjective. What one rider may find difficult, another rider may find easy. Weather conditions, maintenance, and user type also contribute to the great variations in technical difficulty that a trail may exhibit.

Notes on the trail is a more in-depth look at the highlights (and low points) of the ride. The ride descriptions are my impressions of the trail and the ride.

Restrictions are any known restrictions, fees, permits, or closures that may affect your opportunity to ride the trail. The ones listed may not be the current or only restrictions. Use the contact information in the appendices, and *always* check the trailhead information board before you ride.

IMPORTANT: If the trail is located in a wildlife management area (WMA), it may be closed during scheduled hunting days throughout the year. Trust me, you do not want to be on these trails during hunting season! Save yourself a possible long drive by calling the game management section of the Georgia Department of Natural Resources at the number listed in Appendix C. Failure to honor the trail closure policy could result in some nasty consequences!

The Ride is a description of the ride with mileage points at turns and other points of note to give you some orientation. Because there is an unwritten rule somewhere that no two cycle computers can ever exactly match mileage, use common sense when following the mileage points.

The **Elevation Graph** is designed to show you the ride's elevation contour. The slopes depicted are not literal, and the graphs are not to scale.

If you compare them to other graphs in this book, you can get a good idea of the way the ride feels from the bike.

The **Map** is designed to show you the general layout of the trail or loop configuration. Each twist and turn of the trail may not be shown, as well as many of the smaller intersections in the ride description. The map is as accurate as this format allows, but if you're going to orienteer, I would recommend using a topographic map or other assistance.

THE BASICS

Mountain biking is a strenuous and potentially dangerous sport. Use the old Boy Scout motto: Be Prepared! A few basics will make your experience much more enjoyable. Many of these trails are in isolated areas of public or private land, and depending on the season, may be rarely visited. Don't depend on someone to come along if you have a problem—take with you what you may need.

- Riding without a helmet is dangerous and irresponsible. Always wear your skid lid.
- No matter how far you ride, take along a patch kit, spare tube, pump, basic tools such as 3, 4, 5, and 6 mm allen wrenches, standard and phillips screwdrivers, a small adjustable wrench, a small pair of Channel-Locks, a chain tool, and a spoke wrench. That sounds like a lot, but many small tool kits contain most of these tools in a reasonably compact package. I also carry some duct tape and a few extra links of chain with me, both of which have proven invaluable. A seat bag or pack designed to go over a backborne hydration system will easily carry these items.
- Water and food are a given, although you'd be surprised how many novices don't bring either. Energy bars don't take up much room, and you'll be glad you brought them on longer or more difficult rides. Don't ever ride without adequate water. Whether in summer or winter, the exertion of riding a mountain bike can easily dehydrate you. When you first start riding, take more than you think you need. The backpack-style hydration system works well and allows you to keep your hands on the bars.
- A basic first-aid kit is one of those items you hope you won't need, but must have. Many sporting goods outlets carry pre-packaged kits that are small enough to be easily carried along.

Though it seems obvious, the lack of any one of these items can turn an easy ride into an all-day drudge. Inevitably, whenever I forget a patch kit or spare tube, I'll get a flat. If I forget a chain tool, I'll break a chain. If I don't bring some food along, I'll surely bonk halfway up the climb. Moreover, I usually run out of water anyway. Don't tempt the fates!

Riding is a year-round sport in Georgia if you don't mind a little cold, heat, or precipitation. The weather can be unpredictable, though, so take enough extra clothing and basic supplies during cool weather or for an unexpected soaking. I carry an emergency solar blanket and a disposable poncho in my pack—they take up space but it is well worth it. I also wear multiple thin layers of clothing, so that I can easily shed layers as conditions warrant. Many times during winter rides, I'll sweat on the climbs, then be chilled on the downhill. Having a light zip-front jacket as the outer layer allows me to regulate my temperature more easily. Padded shorts or tights are a must, even if you wouldn't wear them into Bubba's Bait Shop to get a postride refresher. Just wear a long T-shirt for the after-ride public appearances. Shoes designed specifically for mountain biking are a must. They generally have stiff soles but allow you to walk in reasonable comfort when the need arises (which is often for me).

You can buy a passable mountain bike for a few hundred dollars—any bike with at least 18 speeds, decent components, tires, and brakes will do. That being said, you will enjoy your ride much more if you have a good bike that is actually designed to be ridden off-road. The more you ride, the better-quality bike you will need. But don't worry about starting out with a less expensive bike. You will quickly find out what parts need to be better and stronger, and attrition will speed you along to your next level of bike, which is actually part of the fun. Your spouse can't deny your replacing a broken part—after all, it's maintenance. Remember, when you buy bikes and components, you get what you pay for.

The price of bike does not a rider make. I've been passed many times on my high-buck full-suspension recliner of a bike by some kid on an entry-level rigid frame. No amount of titanium or gadgetry will offset 20 years of bad habits. So I subscribe to Mike Maness's philosophy about fancy bikes: We may not go very fast, but we look good.

One of the best ways to prevent mechanical mishaps is to thoroughly clean and check your bike after each ride. That's usually when I find broken or close-to-breaking parts. The more you maintain your bike, the less parts will wear prematurely, and the less you will have to replace. Get to know the mechanics at your local bike shop—they are your friend. There's a reason most professional mountain bike racers have professional mechanics on staff—this sport is hard on equipment no matter at what level you ride. Take care of your bike and it will carry you back from those epic rides.

And take care of yourself, too. If it's been a few weeks or months since your last ride and you're a little out of shape, don't do the 26-mile multipeaked mountain ride thinking you can ride yourself back into shape. Very few people I know are that strong. To ride consistently at a certain level, most folks have to build their way up over time. Take time to build a good base of consistent rides before you tackle the longer or more strenuous rides.

It's not a good idea to go on rides in the more remote areas alone. If something happens to you or your bike, the chances of someone coming along to help are less than on the trails in the more populated areas. If you must ride alone, at least tell someone where you're going and when to start really worrying if you don't return. Also be sure to take along the basic tools and supplies.

One more thing: If you're an experienced rider and you introduce friends to the sport, don't take them out and hammer them on a long, rough, strenuous ride—unless they are elite athletes with far superior natural technical skills—or they probably will not ride again. Remember back when you started? Sometimes you don't realize how far you've come until you take a true beginner along. Let folks ease into the sport and they'll become enthusiasts like us.

A FEW SAGE WORDS

- Keep your weight way back when descending steep pitches.
- Keep your weight forward when riding up steep pitches.
- Don't ride with your muscles tense; relax and don't clench the bars.
- You will have to learn to use the front brake effectively to ride technical sections. Practice somewhere safe before you need to use it.
- Look ahead, so you can anticipate what's coming up.
- Don't look where you don't want to go.
- You can't ride everything. Don't be afraid to walk some sections. Discretion is the better part of valor.
- Don't be afraid to try again.
- Stop and enjoy the surroundings. Wave and speak to other riders.
- Don't litter, and pack out any trash you find along the way.
- Remember that this is supposed to be fun; don't take yourself too seriously.
- Follow the IMBA rules of the trail.
- Volunteer. You'll probably enjoy it, and you'll definitely appreciate the trails you ride.

IMBA'S RULES OF THE TRAIL

The International Mountain Bicycling Association (IMBA) is a nonprofit advocacy organization dedicated to promoting mountain biking that's environmentally sound and socially responsible. IMBA's work keeps trails open and in good condition for everyone.

These rules of the trail are reprinted with permission from IMBA.

1. **Ride on open trails only.** Respect trail and road closures (ask if not sure), avoid possible trespass on land, obtain permits and authorization as may be required. Federal and state wilderness areas are closed to cycling. The way you ride will influence trail management decisions and policies.

2. **Leave no trace.** Be sensitive to the dirt beneath you. Even on open (legal) trails, avoid riding immediately after heavy rains or when the trail surface is soft and muddy. In some locations, muddy trails are unavoidable. Recognize different types of soils and trail construction. Practice low-impact cycling. This also means staying on existing trails and not creating new ones. Be sure to pack out at least as much as you pack in.

3. **Control your bicycle.** Inattention for even a second can cause problems. Obey all bicycle speed regulations and recommendations.

4. **Always yield trail.** Give your fellow trail users plenty of advance notice when you're approaching. A friendly greeting (or bell) is considerate and works well; don't startle others. Show your respect when passing by slowing

to a walking pace or even stopping, particularly when you meet horses. Anticipate other trail users around corners or in blind spots.

5. **Don't scare animals.** All animals are startled by an unannounced approach, a sudden movement, or a loud noise. This can be dangerous for you, others, and the animals. Give animals extra room and time to adjust to you. When passing horses use special care and follow the directions from the horseback riders (ask if uncertain). Running cattle and disturbing wildlife is a serious offense. Leave gates as you found them, or as marked.

6. **Plan ahead.** Know your equipment, your ability, and the area in which you are riding—prepare accordingly. Be self-sufficient at all times, keep your equipment in good repair, and carry all necessary supplies for changes in weather or other conditions. A well-executed trip is a satisfaction to you and not a burden or offense to others. Always wear a helmet.

Pigeon Mountain

Pigeon Mountain is located just west of LaFayette, Georgia, in the northwest corner of the state. The mountain resembles a tabletop—the sides steep and the top relatively flat.

The top of the mountain is laced with old roadbeds and trails of various origins, some in great condition and well marked, and others of dubious origin and legality. The level riding is fairly technical because horses are allowed on most of the trails. In wet weather there's nothing messier than a trail on soft dirt after several horses have walked through the softer sections. Nothing against horses—just remember this when you schedule your ride.

Although the trails lie in the Armuchee District of the Chattahoochee-Oconee National Forest, the area is administered as a wildlife management area and is operated by the Georgia Department of Natural Resources (DNR). There is a game check station at the bottom of the road that goes up the mountain, Rocky Way, and hunting schedules should be posted there. Make sure to stop and check the bulletin board before making the drive up, or call the Georgia DNR for schedules and information.

Please remember that the foot trail to Rock Town is for hikers only. Leave your bike along the trail somewhere and take a quick walk to explore the area—it's interesting. Pigeon Mountain is a little farther away from Atlanta than some of the more popular riding areas, but the many trail opportunities make it a worthy destination.

Atwood/West Brow Loop

Location:	About 8 miles west of LaFayette, about 2 hours northwest of Atlanta.
Distance:	13.8 miles.
Time:	3 hours.
Tread:	1.2 miles on gravel road, 1.4 miles on doubletrack, and 11.2 miles on singletrack, some on old roadbed.
Aerobic level:	Strenuous.
Technical difficulty:	4.

Highlights:	Great overlook, creek crossings, technical sections, wildlife.
Land status:	The trails are in the Chattahoochee-Oconee National Forest, Armuchee District. This is a multi-use trail; please respect the rights of other users.
Maps:	USGS LaFayette and Cedar Grove.
Access:	From Atlanta, go north on Interstate 75 to Exit 133 for Georgia Highway 136. Turn left on GA 136 and go 6.8 miles. Turn right at a stop sign, and go 15.2 miles to another stop sign. Turn left and travel 1.4 miles to a right turn at the sign for LaFayette. Go 4.8 miles to GA 193 in downtown LaFayette. Turn left and go 0.3 mile, then turn right at the light. Go 2.9 miles to Chamberlain Road, and turn left. Travel 3.5 miles to Rocky Lane, a gravel road where you will turn right and go 3.8 miles to the overlook and parking area.

Notes on the trail: If you like singletrack and technical sections, you're going to like this trail. With more than 11 miles of singletrack and lots of technical sections along the way, there's enough to keep most riders interested for the entire ride. The climbs are short and steep, and the downhills are shorter and steeper. You will walk at least a couple of sections, unless you're a super mountain biker.

Several wildlife openings and ponds along the way offer lots of opportunities for viewing the local wildlife, and from what I've seen, there's plenty of it here. Keep your eyes open for the slithery type along the rocky sections and creek crossings; there's plenty of those here too.

The trail starts and ends at the Hood Overlook, which is scenic enough to make the drive worthwhile. This ride should satisfy your singletrack cravings.

Restrictions: This trail is located in a wildlife management area. During fall and spring, controlled hunts are held in this area on some days; the trail may be closed during these hunts. Please check the bulletin board at the game check station at the bottom of the mountain, just off Rocky Way, or call the information number listed in Appendix C.

THE RIDE

0.0 Directly across from the overlook is the trailhead, marked by orange blazes. Begin by pedaling north on a dirt roadbed.

0.1 Wildlife opening to the left.

0.3 Singletrack veers left; go left and follow the blazes.

0.5 Stream crossing.

0.8 Intersection with Hood Trail; turn right and follow the blazes.

1.5 Trail turns right toward a gravel road; another trail enters from left. Go right and cross Rocky Lane.

Atwood/West Brow Loop

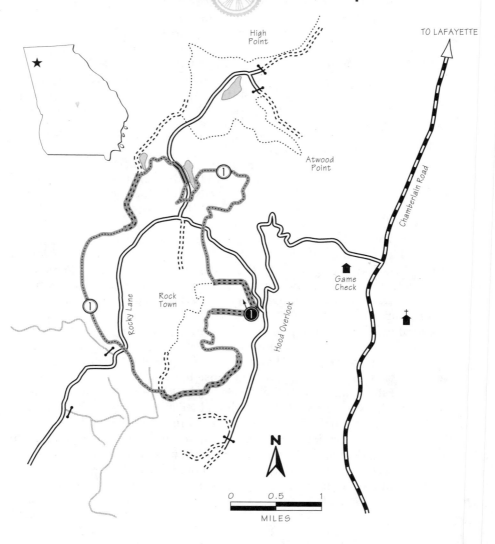

TO LAFAYETTE

High
Point

Atwood
Point

Chamberlain Road

Game
Check

Rock
Town

Rocky Lane

Hood Overlook

N

0   0.5   1

MILES

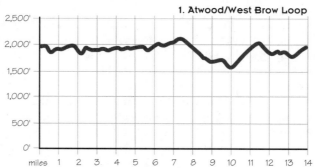

1. Atwood/West Brow Loop

2,500'			
2,000'			
1,500'			
1,000'			
500'			
0'			

miles 1 2 3 4 5 6 7 8 9 10 11 12 13 14

1.8	A blue-blazed trail enters from left; bear right and follow the orange blazes.
2.1	Stream crossing.
3.0	Stream crossing.
3.6	Trail enters from the right; stay on the main trail.
3.8	Several unmarked trails enter from either side; stay on the orange-blazed trail.
3.9	Wildlife opening and pond to the left.
4.0	The trail crosses a dam between ponds, then goes right. Follow the orange blazes.
4.2	Trail intersects gravel McCutchens Spring Road. Bear right, down the hill on the gravel road.
4.4	Road enters from right; stay on the main gravel road.
4.7	Orange blazes turn right off the road; stay straight on the gravel road.
5.0	White-blazed West Brow Trail enters from left at an open area; go left. (Watch for this one: it's easy to miss!)
5.4	Just past a lake and wildlife opening, the green-blazed Bear Lake Trail enters from the left. Go straight, following the white blazes.
5.6	Technical creek crossing.
6.4	Trail bears right; go right and follow the white blazes.
8.8	End of West Brow Trail at a gravel road; turn left and follow the orange blazes.
8.9	Atwood Trail enters from right; go right and follow the orange blazes.
9.0	Roadbed to the left; stay straight on the blazed trail.
9.1	Trail enters from the left; continue on the blazed trail.
9.8	Trail becomes doubletrack.
9.9	Creek crossing; this is Allen Creek.
10.0	Blue-blazed Hood Trail enters from left; stay straight on the orange-blazed trail.

Scenery on the Atwood/West Brow Loop.

10.1 Doubletrack continues straight and Atwood Trail goes left. Go left, following the orange-blazed singletrack.

11.5 Wildlife opening to the left.

12.4 Stream crossing.

12.9 Dirt road enters from left; go right and follow the orange blazes.

13.1 Creek crossing.

13.2 Wildlife opening to the right; trail turns to doubletrack past the wildlife opening.

13.7 Doubletrack intersects a gravel road at a gate; turn left on the gravel road.

13.8 Ride ends at the overlook parking area.

Atwood/Hood Loop

Location:	About 8 miles west of LaFayette, about 2 hours northwest of Atlanta.
Distance:	6 miles.
Time:	1.5 hours.
Tread:	2.5 miles on singletrack, 1.1 miles on doubletrack on old roadbed, and 2.4 miles on gravel road.
Aerobic level:	Moderate.
Technical difficulty:	3.5.
Highlights:	Technical singletrack, creek crossing, overlook.
Land status:	The trail is located in the Chattahoochee-Oconee National Forest, Armuchee District. This is a multi-use trail; please respect the rights of other users.
Maps:	USGS LaFayette and Cedar Grove.
Access:	From Atlanta, go north on Interstate 75 to Exit 133, Georgia Highway 136. Turn left on GA 136 and go 6.8 miles. Turn right at a stop sign, and go 15.2 miles to another stop sign. Turn left and go 1.4 miles to the sign for LaFayette. Turn right and travel 4.8 miles to GA 193 in downtown LaFayette. Turn left and go 0.3 mile, then turn right at the light, and go 2.9 miles to Chamberlain Road; turn left. Go 3.5 miles and turn right on Rocky Lane for 3.8 miles. At the intersection on top of the mountain, turn left and go 0.3 mile to the overlook and parking area.

Notes on the trail: Here's a little shorter version of the Pigeon Mountain ride. Although not as long as the other rides described here, there's no shortage of singletrack to make your ride a great one. There are a few technical

Atwood/Hood Loop
Atwood/Bear Lake Loop

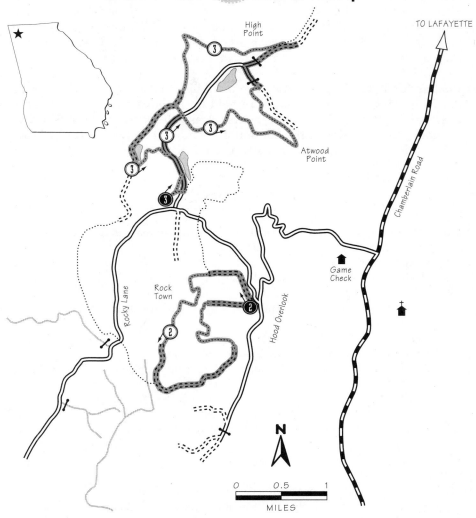

High
Point

TO LAFAYETTE

Atwood
Point

Chamberlain Road

Game
Check

Rock
Town

Rocky Lane

Hood Overlook

N

0   0.5   1

MILES

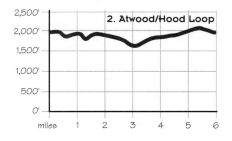

2. Atwood/Hood Loop

2,500'
2,000'
1,500'
1,000'
500'
0'

miles   1   2   3   4   5   6

sections along the way to test your skills (or patience), and at least one down-hill that you just might need to walk. There's enough scenery along the tamer sections of trail to keep your attention even as you recover from the more difficult sections. You can take a short off-bike excursion to Rock Town for some interesting rock formations and scenery, then continue your ride back to the overlook. The trails are well marked, and the blazes are easy to follow. Enjoy.

Restrictions: This trail is located in a wildlife management area. During fall and spring, controlled hunts are held in this area on some days. This trail may be closed during these hunts. Please check the bulletin board at the game check station at the bottom of the mountain, just off Rocky Way, or call the information number listed in Appendix C.

THE RIDE

0.0 Directly across from the overlook is the trailhead, marked by orange blazes. The first section is on a dirt roadbed.
0.1 Wildlife opening to the left.
0.3 Singletrack veers left; go left and follow the blazes.
0.5 Stream crossing.
0.8 Trail intersection; Atwood Trail turns right. Go straight on the blue-blazed Hood Trail.
1.2 Steep downhill.
1.3 Stream crossing; technical climb on the other side.
1.6 Trail intersection; turn left and follow the blue blazes. The trail ahead is closed to bikes.
2.8 Blue-blazed Hood Trail intersects the orange-blazed Atwood Trail. Go left on the Atwood Trail. This section is on an old roadbed.
3.0 Atwood Trail bears left off the roadbed; go straight and stay on the doubletrack.
3.1 Stream crossing.
3.6 Roadbed turns into a gravel road.
3.9 Stream crossing.
4.1 Roadbed enters from the right; stay on the gravel road.
4.2 Intersection with gravel South Brow Road; turn left on South Brow Road.
5.2 Gated wildlife opening to the left.
5.4 Roadbed enters from the left; stay straight on the main gravel road.
5.9 Atwood Trail enters from the left; stay on the main gravel road.
6.0 Ride ends at the overlook parking area.

Atwood/Bear Lake Loop

See Map on Page 13	
Location:	About 8 miles west of LaFayette, about 2 hours northwest of Atlanta.
Distance:	9.6 miles.
Time:	2 hours.
Tread:	1.9 miles on gravel road, 2.3 miles on old doubletrack, and 5.4 miles on singletrack.
Aerobic level:	Moderate.
Technical difficulty:	3.5.
Highlights:	Technical singletrack, lakes, highest local point.
Land status:	The trail is located in the Chattahoochee-Oconee National Forest, Armuchee District. This is a multi-use trail; please respect the rights of other users.
Maps:	USGS LaFayette and Cedar Grove.
Access:	From Atlanta, go north on Interstate 75 to Exit 133 for Georgia Highway 136. Turn left on GA 136 and travel 6.8 miles to a stop sign; go 15.2 miles to another stop sign. Turn left and go 1.4 miles to the sign for LaFayette. Turn right and go 4.8 miles to GA 193 in downtown LaFayette. Turn left and go 0.3 mile, then turn right at the light, 2.9 miles to Chamberlain Road; turn left. Drive 3.5 miles to Rocky Lane; turn right and go 3.8 miles. At the intersection on top of the mountain, turn right and travel 1.5 miles to McCutchens Spring Road. Turn right and go 0.2 mile to a parking area on the left.

Notes on the trail: Here is yet another of the many combinations of trails you can use to create rides on Pigeon Mountain. This loop uses parts of three trails, with three different colored blazes along the route to further confuse you. The blazed trails are well marked, so don't let the description fool you. The trails are easy to follow. Part of this trail goes near High Point, the aptly named highest point in the immediate area at 2,215 feet. That doesn't sound like much, but when you factor in the dramatic slopes of the mountain, it seems higher.

An intermediate distance of 9.6 miles gives you lots of opportunity to hone your singletrack skills. There are a couple technical sections along the way just in case you get bored with all that singletrack. Take your time and enjoy the area.

Restrictions: This trail is located in a wildlife management area. During fall and spring, controlled hunts are held in this area on some days. This trail may be closed during these hunts. Please check the bulletin board at the game check station at the bottom of the mountain, just off Rocky Way, or call the information number listed in Appendix C.

THE RIDE

0.0 From the parking area, go left on McCutchens Spring Road.

0.1 Orange-blazed Atwood Trail enters from the right; stay on the gravel road.

0.2 Lake to the right, gate just ahead; go straight.

0.7 Orange-blazed Atwood Trail enters from the right; go right, onto the singletrack.

1.3 Trail intersection. Go right, following the orange blazes.

1.5 Stream crossing. Just uphill from the stream crossing is an intersection; bear left on the orange-blazed trail.

2.2 Trail intersection. Go right, following the orange blazes. The trail joins a roadbed.

3.4 Trail intersects another roadbed. Turn left, following the orange blazes.

4.5 Gate across the roadbed; just past the gate the road turns to gravel. Go straight.

4.8 Intersection with another gravel road; turn right.

4.9 Gate across the road; continue straight on the doubletrack. The orange blazes continue.

5.2 Wildlife opening to the left.

5.3 Intersection. Turn left and follow the blue and white blazes.

6.5 Wildlife opening to the left; High Point to the right.

7.3 Trail intersection. The blue-blazed Pocket Trail enters from the right; go left, following the white blazes.

7.7 Trail joins a gravel roadbed; bear right onto the roadbed, following the white blazes. Wildlife opening to the right.

7.9 Bear right off the gravel road onto the white blazed singletrack West Brow Trail.

8.3 Trail intersection near a lake. Turn left onto the green-blazed Bear Lake Trail.

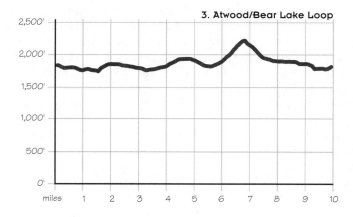

Easy does it . . .

8.4 Trail intersects a doubletrack road; bear right onto the roadbed. Look for the green blazes.

8.7 Trail intersection. Turn left, following the green blazes.

8.9 Bear Lake Trail ends at a gate at McCutchens Spring Road; turn right onto the gravel road.

9.4 Lake to the left.

9.5 Orange-blazed Atwood Trail enters from the left; stay on the gravel road.

9.6 Ride ends at the parking lot.

The Cohutta District

The Chattahoochee-Oconee National Forest's Cohutta District lies in the northwest section of the contiguous forest, just to the east of Georgia Highway 411. The Cohutta District contains some of the oldest and best mountain bike trails in the state. The district management's early progressive approach to developing mountain bike trails has been a great example of cooperative trail development between the USDA Forest Service and user groups. Many of the Southern Off-Road Bicycle Association's (SORBA) long-time members learned much of the fine art of trail building here, from some of the best teachers in the country, Mike Davis and Larry Thomas (who, incidentally, still teach me a thing or two every time I work with them).

Classic rides like Bear Creek, Mountaintown Creek, and Windy Gap, and newer classics-to-be like the recently opened Iron Mountain/Conasauga River Loop and the Sumac Creek Trail give testament to the extent of the district's commitment to quality trails.

The Cohutta District is also where access groups like SORBA are learning the fine art of volunteer organization, motivation, and appreciation. The district's extremely successful volunteer program is a model for programs everywhere, and the Cohutta Volunteers are a great and diverse group of motivated people.

You can spend a lot of time exploring the trails in this district, and I can't think of even one that is not worth the trip.

Iron Mountain Loop (Winter Loop)

Location:	8 miles east of Cisco, about 2 hours north of Atlanta, and 1 hour south of Chattanooga, Tennessee.
Distance:	8.5 miles.
Time:	2.5 hours.
Tread:	4.4 miles on gravel forest road, and 4.1 miles on singletrack, some on old roadbeds.
Aerobic level:	Moderate.

Iron Mountain Loop (Winter Loop)

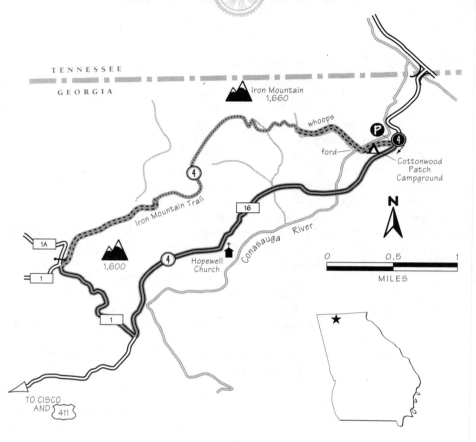

TENNESSEE

GEORGIA

Iron Mountain
1,660

whoops

P

ford

Cottonwood
Patch
Campground

4

Iron Mountain Trail

16

Conasauga River

1A

1,600

4

Hopewell
Church

1

1

N

0   0.5   1

MILES

TO CISCO
AND 411

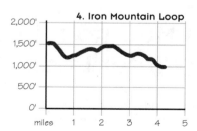

4. Iron Mountain Loop

2,000'

1,500'

1,000'

500'

0'

miles   1   2   3   4   5

Technical difficulty:	2.5. Wet weather can change this ride into a slick, treacherous fall-fest on some sections. Use caution!
Highlights:	A small river ford, dozer-built water bar launching pads, forested singletrack, and great views.
Land status:	This trail is located within the Chattahoochee-Oconee National Forest, Cohutta District. This is a multi-use trail; please respect the rights of other users.
Maps:	USGS Tennga.
Access:	From Atlanta, follow Interstate 75 north to Exit 126 for U.S. Highway 411. Follow US 411 north through several small towns, approximately 51 miles to Cisco. Look for a rock church on the right, and Greg's Store on the left. Turn right on old Georgia Highway 2, at the Sumac Creek Shooting Range sign. At 1.6 miles, the road forks; take the right fork. About 0.3 mile farther is another branch; take the middle route. Go 5.6 miles, bear left at a fork, and you will see Cottonwood Patch Campground on your left. There is a separate gravel parking area next to the camping area.

Notes on the trail: This configuration of the Iron Mountain Trail is an easier winter loop of forest roads and singletrack. The loop includes a moderate climb on a gravel forest road, which deposits you at the trailhead with 4.5 miles of singletrack ahead of you. The ride ends with a refreshing ford through the Conasauga River just below the finish point. On a hot day this ford is perfect for a postride cool-down.

The first half of the loop is on gravel forest and county roads. The second half is mostly singletrack, with a series of short downhills depositing you at the river crossing. An opening in the trees along one ridge affords views of the surrounding hills. A section of the trail runs through a dense old pine forest, where the whispered sounds of your passing are hushed by the ground cover. In fall, the hardwood forested ridges offer excellent leaf-watching. The series of dozer-built water bars on the last downhill make great launching pads.

Restrictions: There is a $2 day-use fee for this trail.

THE RIDE

0.0 From Cottonwood Patch, pedal back along County Road 103/Forest Road 16 for 3.1 miles.

3.1 Turn right on Forest Road 1 and go uphill. Enjoy the climb!

4.4 Iron Mountain Trailhead is to the right, just before a gate at the intersection of FR 1 and FR 1A. Turn right and follow the first section of trail, running parallel to another forest road on the left for the first few hundred feet. The trail follows an old woods roadbed.

Huffin' and Puffin' in North Georgia.

5.4 Singletrack begins.

7.6 Trail intersection; go straight.

8.4 Ford the Conasauga River.

8.5 Ride ends at the Cottonwood Patch Campground.

Iron Mountain/Conasauga River Loop (Summer Loop)

Location: About 8 miles east of Cisco, about 2 hours from Atlanta.

Distance: 11.8 miles.

Time: 2.75 hours.

Tread: 3.8 miles on singletrack on old railroad bed, 3.7 miles on singletrack, 2.9 miles on gated forest road, and 1.5 miles on open gravel forest or county roads.

Aerobic level: Moderately strenuous.

Technical difficulty: 3, except for the river ford, which could rate up to a 5 in certain conditions.

Highlights: Beautiful views, a small and a large river fording, sweet singletrack sidehill, and a great downhill with jumps.

Land status: The Georgia section of the trail is located in the Chattahoochee-Oconee National Forest, Cohutta District. The Tennessee section of the trail is located in the Cherokee National Forest, Oconee Ranger District. This is a multi-use trail; please respect the rights of other users.

Maps: USGS for the Georgia section of trail is Tennga; for the Tennessee section USGS Parksville.

Access: From Atlanta, follow Interstate 75 north to Exit 126 for U.S. Highway 411. Follow US 411 north through several small towns, approximately 51 miles to Cisco. Look for a rock church on the right and Greg's Store on the left. Turn right on old Georgia Highway 2, at the Sumac Creek Shooting Range sign. At 1.6 miles, the road forks; take the right fork. About 0.3 mile farther is another branch—take the middle route; 5.6 miles farther, bear left at another fork; you will see Cottonwood Patch Campground on your left. There is a separate gravel parking area next to the camping area.

Iron Mountain/Conasauga River Loop
(Summer Loop)

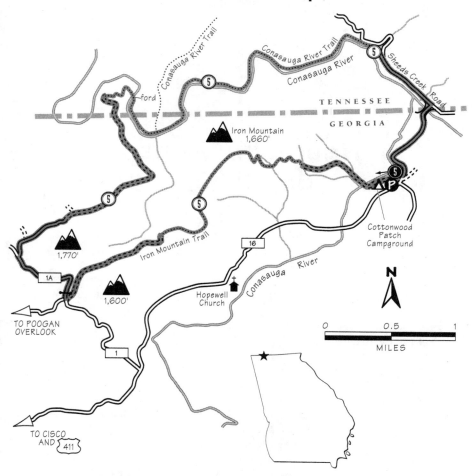

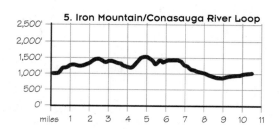

5. Iron Mountain/Conasauga River Loop

Notes on the trail: The connecting trail from the Iron Mountain Trail to the Conasauga River Trail creates a challenging warm-weather loop opportunity. The connector trail includes sidehill singletrack and an exhilarating downhill, with a river fording thrown in for good measure. The trail crosses the state line and travels in Tennessee for several miles. The last section of the Conasauga River Trail runs on an old timber railroad bed along the banks of the Conasauga River for just over 4 miles. The grade is minimal, and this section makes an excellent, easy out-and-back from the opposite direction.

The section along the river in Tennessee is beautiful, with several stopping places to gaze upon the river, or fish, or skip rocks. The sidehill singletrack approach to the river is freshly cut, and the preceding downhill is one of the better ones in this area. There is an overlook on the gated fire road that opens in three directions, giving beautiful vistas of the Cohuttas, and views into Tennessee.

You can take an unscheduled swim at the river ford and find out just how waterproof your sealed components are—I did. Plan on getting wet in the best of conditions!

Warning! *Do not attempt to ford the Conasauga River after heavy rains or during extended rainy periods! The current is deceptively strong, and the ford can be treacherous to anyone on foot. It is not rideable on a bicycle.* Please check with the USDA Forest Service if you have any questions on the conditions.

Restrictions: There is a $2 day-use fee for this trail.

THE RIDE

0.0 From the Cottonwood Patch Campground pedal west on the old roadbed.

0.1 Ford the Conasauga River (this is not the ford the warning applies to). Just across the river follow a trail on an old roadbed.

0.9 Trail intersection; go straight.

1.3 Overlook to the left.

3.1 Singletrack ends at the roadbed; continue on the roadbed up the hill.

4.1 Gate at gravel Forest Road 1. Make a sharp right turn and follow the gated road, Forest Road 1A, that parallels the trail you just rode up.

4.8 Forest road enters from the right; turn right.

6.1 Scenic overlook. Enjoy!

7.0 Singletrack begins.

7.5 Sharp switchback right onto an old roadbed. Just downslope is the Conasauga ford. Use caution here! After you ford the river, take the trail to the right.

7.7 Conasauga River Trail enters from the left. Go straight.

8.7 Stream crossing.

9.2 Double stream crossing.

9.3 Stream crossing. (And you thought your feet were going to dry out.)

9.8 Stream crossing.

10.0 Stream crossing.

10.3 Stream crossing and trailhead. Enter a gravel parking area.

10.4 Road from the parking area joins Sheed's Creek Road. Bear right.

11.0 At the intersection, turn right and cross the iron bridge back over the Conasauga River.

11.8 Turn right into Cottonwood Patch Campground.

Sumac Creek Loop

Location: About 5 miles west of Cisco, 2 hours north of Atlanta and 1 hour from Chattanooga, Tennessee.

Distance: 10.8 miles for the described loop. A figure-eight option increases the distance to 14.4 miles.

Time: 2 hours for the loop.

Tread: 1.7 miles on singletrack, 5.6 miles on singletrack trail on old forest roadbed, and 3.5 miles on gated forest road.

Aerobic level: Moderate.

Technical difficulty: 3.5. The first mile is rocky and loose from being freshly cut. The trail should eventually wear to about a level 3.

Highlights: Views along the ridgelines, two creek crossings, switchbacks, great singletrack, and good bear potential.

Land status: This trail is located within the Chattahoochee-Oconee National Forest, Cohutta District. This is a multi-use trail; please respect the rights of other users.

Maps: USGS Tennga.

Access: From Atlanta, go north on Interstate 75 to Exit 126 for U.S. Highway 411 north. Follow US 411 north through Chatsworth. Approximately 13 miles north of Chatsworth, look for Greg's General Store on your left, near a sign for Cisco. Just across from Greg's Store is old Georgia Highway 2, beside a stone church. Turn right on GA 2. At 1.5 miles, the road forks; go right. At 1.8 miles, go straight at a three-way intersection. After 3.1 miles, turn right on Forest Road 17, across from a game check cabin on your left. Follow FR 17 2.1 miles to a parking lot on your right at the intersection of FR 17 and FR 17A. Park here. The trailhead is about 0.1 mile down FR 17A on

Sumac Creek Loop

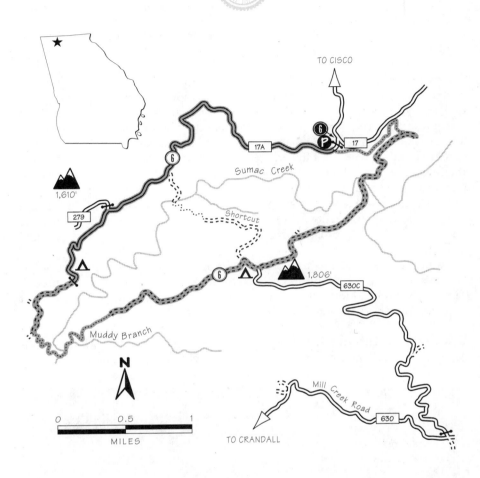

TO CISCO

Sumac Creek

Shortcut

1,610'

279

1,806'

630C

Muddy Branch

Mill Creek Road

TO CRANDALL

630

N

0   0.5   1

MILES

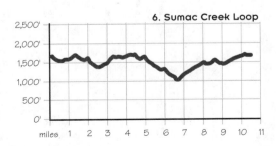

6. Sumac Creek Loop

2,500'
2,000'
1,500'
1,000'
500'
0'

miles 1 2 3 4 5 6 7 8 9 10 11

your left. As an alternative, continue along FR 17 another 5.2 miles to the intersection with FR 630. Turn right and travel for 1.6 miles to the intersection with FR 630C on your right and FR 630A on your left. Go left 0.7 mile to another gravel parking area for a longer loop.

Notes on the trail: The trail follows two parallel ridgelines, with a dip at either end to cross Sumac Creek. The views along the ridgelines are great and give you a good excuse to stop often. There are some pretty spots down along the creek that just beg for a camera and a few minutes of exploration. The creek crossings are deep and refreshing. If you like switchbacks, you'll love this trail. If you don't like switchbacks, at least you'll be better at riding them when you're finished. The climbs are typical Cohutta—short but steep— and you have to earn the three overlooks. Fall colors are awesome through- out the trail. I saw several fresh bear signs here during our first ride. There is a sweet singletrack downhill halfway through the ride that makes the ensuing climb out almost worth it. This is one of the most well-marked trails I've ridden.

Sumac Creek Trail was completed October 3, 1997; a joint project of the USDA Forest Service, Cohutta District, SORBA, and the Cohutta Volunteers. The trail can be ridden either as the loop described, or a longer figure eight by using the short through-trail in the middle of the ride.

Restrictions: This trail is located within the Cohutta Wildlife Management Area. During fall, controlled deer hunting is held in this area on certain days

Better to walk than attempt to ride across a bridge like this.

and the trails may be closed. The hunting dates are posted on bulletin boards at game check stations and trailheads; call the number listed in Appendix C for more information.

THE RIDE

0.0 From the parking lot, follow gated FR 17A 0.1 mile to the trailhead on left; turn left. Singletrack begins.

1.1 Five-way intersection. Take the far right branch on the forest roadbed, down the hill.

1.4 Trail enters from the left at a switchback right; stay right.

1.8 Short mud bog at a hard right turn.

2.0 Creek crossing.

2.1 Large creek crossing. Look upstream for a great picture! Trail begins to climb.

3.2 Wildlife opening.

3.6 Intersection with FR 630C at a gravel clearing. Go right through the gate (3.4 miles to the left is an intersection with FR 630. Across that intersection 0.7 mile is another parking area and possible access point).

3.7 Trail forks. Stay left for the loop. (For the figure eight, turn right and go 1.8 miles. When the trail intersects FR 17A, turn left and ride the second half of the ride described here in reverse.)

4.6 Small clearing.

5.3 Singletrack downhill begins. Sweet!

5.8 Creek crossing (this one's deep!). Immediately across the creek, the trail climbs through a series of switchbacks on an old logging roadbed.

6.9 Overlook to the right. See what you earned with that climb?

7.2 Trail enters a group camping area through a gate. Follow gravel FR 17A to the left from this clearing.

8.0 Road enters from the left; go straight.

8.7 Shortcut trail enters from the right.

9.5 Overlook to the right.

10.4 Overlook to the right.

10.7 Trailhead on the right; stay on FR 17A.

10.8 Return to the parking area.

Rocky Flats Loop

Location:	About 8 miles northeast of Chatsworth, 2 hours north of Atlanta.
Distance:	The complete loop is 6.2 miles.
Time:	1.5 hours.
Tread:	5 miles on jeep roads and 1.2 miles on gravel forest road.
Aerobic level:	Moderately easy.
Technical difficulty:	Easy.
Highlights:	Good views from the ridges, easy climbs, and great downhill.
Land status:	The trail lies within the Chattahoochee-Oconee National Forest, Cohutta District. This is a multi-use trail; please respect the rights of other users.
Maps:	USGS Tennga.
Access:	From Atlanta, go north on Interstate 75 to Exit 126 for U.S. Highway 411 north. Follow US 411 north through Chatsworth. About 6 miles north of Chatsworth, turn right at the sign for Crandall. Go about 0.4 mile, cross the railroad tracks, turn right and then immediately left, following the sign to Lake Conasauga. Go about 4 miles on Mill Creek Road, Forest Road 630, bypassing the first Rocky Flats Road sign and continuing to the second Rocky Flats turnoff to the right. Just across the creek is a parking area.

Notes on the trail: Rocky Flats is a loop ride consisting of several varieties of mountain roads. Start with the semirocky but easily rideable first section that climbs gently from the main road. As you progress, the road gradually deteriorates into a narrower but still easily rideable doubletrack. Later on you start to notice large mud holes and fewer routes around them, and the road regresses even more, into a piny jeep trail along the ridge. As you start to descend, the trail turns into an ORV (off-road vehicle) course, becoming more technical, until the last pitch before the creek crossing threatens to launch you right into the creek. Luckily, it looks considerably worse than it is, and the creek crossing, while deep, is easy.

Once through the creek, rejoin the forest road for a short ride back up to the parking area.

Because of the progression of difficulty, this ride is good for teaching a beginner real-world biking skills. The difficulty increases gradually but doesn't get unmanageable.

Rocky Flats Loop

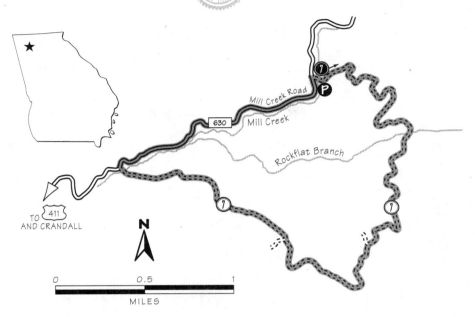

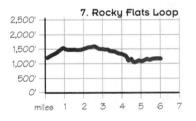

This ride is also good for less-than-perfect weather. The road bed is solid clay or gravel, and the only creek crossing of any significance is at the end.

We saw deer in the woods along the road, as well as signs of other wildlife, human and otherwise. The trail is open to ORVs, so don't be surprised to pass or be passed by a jeep or four-wheeler. As you get closer to the end, you'll have the advantage over motorized users on the technical terrain. The other users we've encountered here have been friendly and helpful.

THE RIDE

0.0 From the parking area, follow the roadbed up the hill, away from FR 630.
0.2 Trail forks left; stay right on the main road.
0.6 Another trail forks left around a gate; stay right.
0.8 Trail enters from the left; go straight.
1.2 Trail crosses; continue straight.
1.4 Creek crossing.
2.0 Trail enters from the left; go straight.

2.1 Trail enters from the left; bear right.

2.4 Clearing on the ridgetop; road bears left.

2.5 Creek crossing.

2.6 Road enters from the right; bear left.

2.8 Road enters from the left; bear right.

3.0 Road enters from the left; go straight.

3.6 Road turns sharp right at an intersection; the road ahead is gated and blocked with a tree.

4.5 Enter a clearcut.

4.9 Creek crossing after a steep downhill section. The trail forks across the creek; go left up to the gravel forest road.

5.0 Rejoin gravel FR 630; go right.

6.2 Turn right, back to the parking area.

Bear Creek Trail and Loop

Location:	9 miles west of Ellijay, about 2 hours from Atlanta.
Distance:	The complete loop with the overlook is 14.7 miles.
Time:	2.5 hours.
Tread:	3.1 miles on singletrack, 6.9 miles trail on roadbed, and 4.7 miles on gravel forest road.
Aerobic level:	Moderate.
Technical difficulty:	3. The creek crossings are tricky!
Highlights:	Great overlook, a huge tree known as the Gennett Poplar, lots of creek frontage, wide-open return descent.
Land status:	The trail is located in the Chattahoochee-Oconee National Forest, Cohutta District. This is a multi-use trail; please respect the rights of other users.
Maps:	USGS Dyer.
Access:	From Atlanta, follow Interstate 75 north to I-575 north. Stay on I-575; it will change to Georgia Highway 515. Follow GA 515 to East Ellijay. At the traffic light next to the Hardee's, turn left on GA 52, and go across the bridge. Just across the bridge, turn left again and continue until you reach the square. Go across the square and turn right, following GA 52 west. After 5 miles look for a sign on your right for Mt. Zion Church. Shortly after the sign, turn right onto a paved road near the bottom of the hill just

Bear Creek Trail and Loop

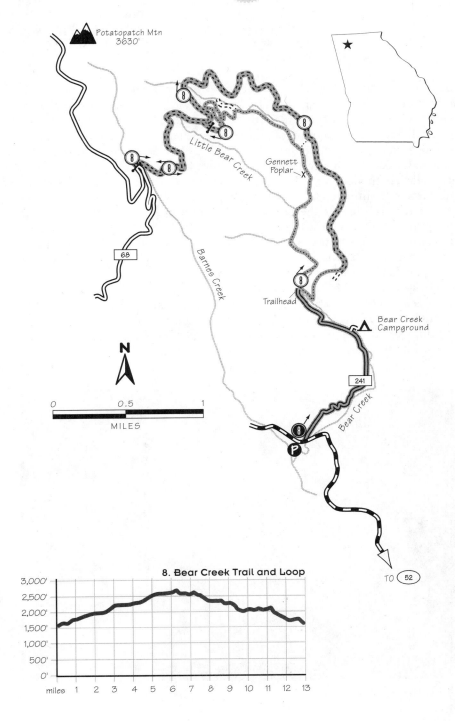

Potatopatch Mtn
3630'

Little Bear Creek

Gennett
Poplar

Barnes Creek

68

Trailhead

Bear Creek
Campground

241

Bear Creek

N

0   0.5   1
MILES

P

TO 52

8. Bear Creek Trail and Loop

3,000'
2,500'
2,000'
1,500'
1,000'
500'
0'

miles 1   2   3   4   5   6   7   8   9   10   11   12   13

before a turn. There is a small brown Forest Service sign on the left. Go 4.8 miles. Just after you cross a bridge, you will see a sign on the right for Bear Creek Campground, next to a gravel Forest Service road. Park just past the gravel road on the right. There is a wide shoulder and the paved road is not well traveled.

Notes on the trail: Bear Creek Trail is one of my favorites! In any season, the surroundings are beautiful. The lower, first section of trail runs along Bear Creek, crossing back and forth several times. The creek is noisy and beautiful, and the surrounding forest is dense and almost primeval. At mile 2.9 take a gander at the Gennett Poplar. This old tree's immense size gives you a good idea of what the forest must have been like before the area was logged earlier this century. The fading roadbed that the trail follows is one of the few remaining signs of that logging.

Once the trail leaves the creek, it climbs on open forest roadbed, with mostly moderate grades. The extra effort to get to the overlook is well rewarded with a view of the surrounding mountains, and a great view of Fort Mountain in the distance. If you look off to your left from the overlook in the valley far below, you can see part of the road you drove in on. The knowledge that the ride back is mostly downhill makes the view even sweeter.

The descent on the return loop is a wide, open, gated forest roadbed with the singletrack line conveniently worn in for you. Put it on autopilot and hang on. One last steep downhill, and a technical creek crossing before the parking lot will wash any pesky bear scat off the bikes. Check out the campground on your way out.

Bear Creek Trail creek crossing.

Bear Creek Loop.

Restrictions: This trail is located in a wildlife management area. During fall and spring, controlled hunting is held in this area on certain days. The trail is closed during these posted hunting days. Please check the bulletin board at the trailhead before you ride the trail, or call the information number listed in Appendix C.

Because the listed forest roads are open to motorized vehicles, watch out for oncoming traffic! There is a $2 day-use fee for this trail. The collection box is located at the trailhead, at the end of the gravel forest road.

THE RIDE

0.0 From the paved road, ride up the gravel forest road about 1.5 miles. The road forks; take the left fork (the right fork leads to the campground).

2.0 Trailhead next to the bulletin board at the upper end of the parking lot.

2.2 Creek crossing.

2.5 Creek crossing.

2.7 Creek crossing.

2.9 The Gennett Poplar—awesome!

3.0 Stream crossing.

3.1 Stream crossing. Just past the stream crossing, the trail forks. Stay left (the right fork is a shortcut to the return loop).

3.2 Creek crossing.

3.3 Stream crossing.

3.7 Sharp switchback left. Trail leaves the creek.

4.4 Wildlife opening; trail turns right.

4.6 Wildlife opening.

4.7 Gate at Forest Road 68. Turn left and follow the gated forest road. (For an early bailout, go right. This is the return loop.)

6.1 Cross Little Bear Creek.

6.2 Gate at FR 68. Turn right. (This road is open to motorized traffic.)

6.5 Overlook. Enjoy the view! When you've seen enough, backtrack down to the gate at mile 4.7 above.

8.3 Back at the gate where the trail enters. To complete the loop, bear left and follow the roadbed.

9.3 Wildlife opening; continue through the gate to your left.

9.6 Road forks; go right.

10.6 Shortcut from the lower trail enters from the right.

10.7 Wildlife opening.

11.5 Wildlife opening.

11.8 Wildlife opening. Trail is to the right. Steep singletrack downhill begins.

12.2 Stream joins trail for a few yards.

12.3 Creek crossing back to parking lot at the trailhead. Turn left and retrace your tracks on FR 241.

14.7 Ride ends at the paved road.

Mountaintown Creek Trail

Location:	9 miles west of Ellijay, about 2 hours from Atlanta.
Distance:	The trail is 5.8 miles long. The combined Bear Creek/Mountaintown Creek Loop option is 22.8 miles.
Time:	1.5 hours for the trail and 3.5 hours for the loop.
Tread:	5.8 miles on singletrack on old logging roadbed.
Aerobic level:	Moderate. The loop option is strenuous.
Technical difficulty:	4.
Highlights:	Numerous technical creek crossings, a long technical downhill, and incredible scenery.
Land status:	The trail is located in the Chattahoochee-Oconee National Forest, Cohutta District. This is a multi-use trail; please respect the rights of other users.
Maps:	USGS Dyer.
Access:	From Atlanta, follow Interstate 75 north to I-575 north. Stay on I-575; it will change to Georgia Highway 515. Continue on GA 515 to East Ellijay. At the traffic light next to the Hardee's, turn left and go

Mountaintown Creek Trail

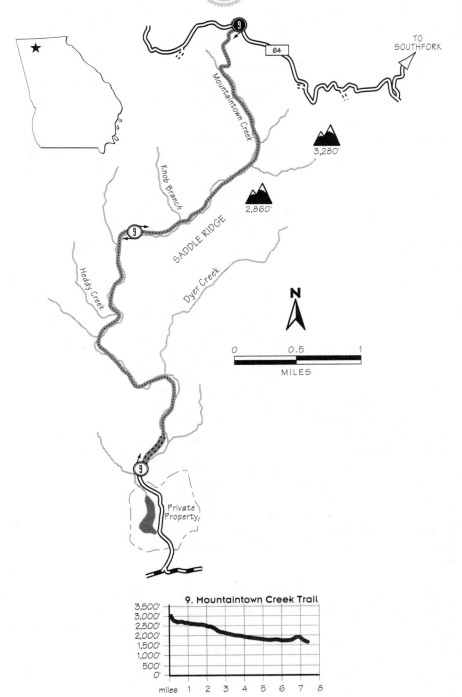

TO SOUTHFORK

64

Mountaintown Creek

Knob Branch

3,280'

2,860'

SADDLE RIDGE

Heddy Creek

Dyer Creek

N

0   0.5   1
MILES

Private Property

9. Mountaintown Creek Trail

3,500'
3,000'
2,500'
2,000'
1,500'
1,000'
500'
0'

miles 1 2 3 4 5 6 7 8

across the bridge. At the next light turn left and drive to the square. Go across the square and turn right, following Georgia Highway 52 west. After 5 miles, look for a sign on your right for Mt. Zion Church then turn right onto a paved road near the bottom of the hill just before a turn. There is a small brown Forest Service sign on the left. Go about 5 miles, passing the entrance to Bear Creek Trail on your right, to Holly Creek Gap Road, Forest Road 90, which enters from the right at the end of the pavement. Turn right and travel about 1.7 miles to Potato Patch Road, FR 68. Turn right and go to the top of the mountain, about 3.3 miles, to the junction with Three Forks Road, FR 64. Turn right and follow the ridge about 7.1 miles to the trailhead on your right.

A great ride option on this trail is to follow the directions to Bear Creek Trail (Ride 8) and park there, incorporating Bear Creek Trail into the loop, or park in the gravel parking lot just past the overlook on Potato Patch Road, and ride the loop from there. Do not park at the Barnes Creek Picnic area!

Notes on the trail: Mountaintown Creek Trail is a classic. It is also one of the wettest rides in northern Georgia. The first 6 miles are singletrack downhill on an old logging roadbed (though you can't always tell), with numerous technical creek crossings. Your feet will get wet! The trail follows Mountaintown Creek for most of its way, until the last few miles, which are on a gravel forest road. If you like the primeval feeling that being in deep woods brings, you'll like Mountaintown. Combining this trail with the Bear Creek Trail to make a loop creates a longtime local favorite.

You'll get some skills practice on this trail. Some of the creek crossings are rideable, some aren't, and the fun is finding out which is which. The creek is surrounded by deep mountain vegetation, and even though you're traveling much of the time on an old logging roadbed, you feel like you're in a virgin forest. Several sections are steep and loose, and discretion seems the better part of valor in at least one spot. The trail can be downright treacherous in wet weather. The trail is mostly downhill except for the last couple miles. Sighting deer, turkey, and even the occasional bear is always a possibility. There are some great photo opportunities along the many small waterfalls. This is a great trail to test chain lubes on!

Restrictions: This trail is located in a wildlife management area. During fall and spring hunting seasons, the trail may be closed. Please check the bulletin board at the trailhead before you ride the trail, or call the number listed in Appendix C.

0.0 Enter the trail at the marked trailhead. The trail starts immediately downhill.

0.5 Trail turns sharp left, toward the creek.

1.2 Creek crossing.

1.3 Creek crossing.

1.5 Creek crossing.

1.6 Creek crossing.

1.7 Steep technical section.

1.9 Creek crossing.

2.3 Creek crossing.

2.8 Creek crossing.

3.0 Creek crossing.

3.1 Stream crossing (just for a change.)

3.3 Creek crossing.

3.6 Creek crossing.

3.7 Creek crossing.

4.0 Double creek crossing.

4.2 Creek crossing.

4.7 Creek crossing.

5.1 Creek crossing.

5.6 Creek crossing.

5.8 Trail ends at the beginning of a roadbed.

Note: To complete the Bear Creek/Mountaintown Creek Loop, continue on the gravel roadbed for 2 miles. Part of the gravel road runs through private property, so stay on the road. At the paved road, turn right; the Bear Creek Trail entrance is just across the bridge to the right.

10

Windy Gap Trail and Loop

Location:	4 miles east of Eton, about 2 hours north of Atlanta.
Distance:	12.9 miles.
Time:	3 hours.
Tread:	0.9 mile on gravel forest road, and 12 miles on ORV trail and doubletrack.
Aerobic level:	Strenuous.
Technical difficulty:	5.

Windy Gap Trail and Loop

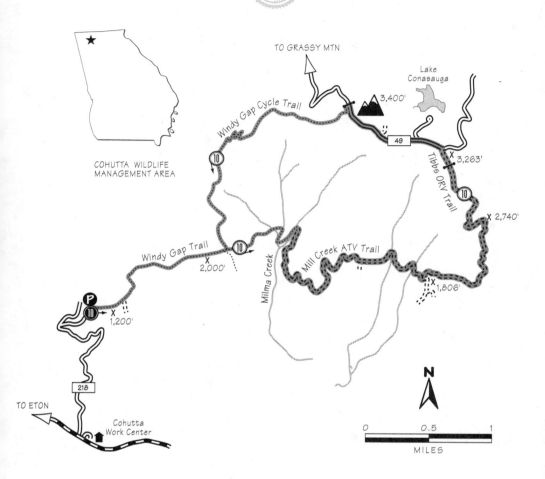

TO GRASSY MTN

Lake
Conasauga

Windy Gap Cycle Trail

3,400'

49

Tibbs ORV Trail

X 3,263'

X 2,740'

COHUTTA WILDLIFE
MANAGEMENT AREA

Windy Gap Trail

X
2,000'

Milma Creek

Mill Creek ATV Trail

X
1,806'

P

X
1,200'

218

TO ETON

Cohutta
Work Center

N

0   0.5   1

MILES

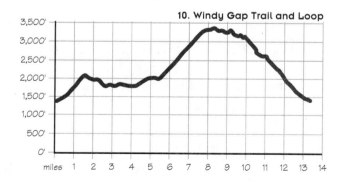

10. Windy Gap Trail and Loop

3,500'
3,000'
2,500'
2,000'
1,500'
1,000'
500'
0'

miles 1 2 3 4 5 6 7 8 9 10 11 12 13 14

	Highlights:	Great views, killer climbs, killer downhills, mucho technical challenge.

Highlights: Great views, killer climbs, killer downhills, mucho technical challenge.

Land status: The trail lies within the Chattahoochee-Oconee National Forest, Cohutta District. This is a multi-use trail and open to motorcycles and ATVs; please respect the rights of other users.

Maps: USGS Crandall.

Access: From Atlanta, go north on Interstate 75 to exit 126 for U.S. Highway 411. Go north on US 411 to Eton, about 4 miles north of Chatsworth. In Eton, turn right at the light onto CCC Camp Road. Go 1.5 miles and where the road forks turn left, which is still CCC Camp Road. Continue 2.7 miles until you see a Forest Service sign on the left beside a gravel forest road. Turn left and follow Forest Road 218 about 2 miles to the parking lot at the trailhead.

Notes on the trail: This is the most technically difficult ride in this book. The combination of the technical terrain and the technical challenges left by the frequent ORV use make this a truly technically nasty fun-fest. Making things even more fun is the brutal climb up the Tibbs ORV Trail to get to the upper trailhead. That climb is my least favorite of all these rides. It just isn't fun at all!

Once on top of the mountain along gravel Forest Road 49, however, the views are spectacular. Just as you enter the singletrack you'll see a warning sign for the trail—the only sign of its kind I have encountered on these trails. As you negotiate the reasons for the sign, the views get even better as you travel back down the Windy Gap section, though you can't safely take your eyes off the trail long enough to see much.

Finishing this one rates high on the satisfaction scale. Much more difficult than the distance would suggest, this is one for the hammerheads!

THE RIDE

0.0 From the parking lot at the lower Windy Gap Trailhead, ride up Windy Gap Trail.

0.3 Unmarked trail enters from the right; stay on the main trail.

1.3 Go right on the Milma Creek ATV Trail.

2.3 Stream crossing. The trail gets fairly technical from this point on.

2.4 Stream crossing.

2.7 Roadbed improves to gravel. This is still an ORV trail, also labeled as FR 78C on some maps.

3.2 Great views of Fort Mountain.

3.5 The roadbed again deteriorates into more technical rocky fun.

4.5 Roadbed enters from the right; go straight on the ORV trail.

4.6 Roadbed and stream join for some sections.

5.1 Wildlife opening to the right.

5.4 Milma Creek Trail ends at the intersection with Tibbs ORV Trail, which goes uphill left, then straight ahead and slightly downhill. Go left on the Tibbs Trail, uphill.

5.5 Stream crossing. The trail gets steadily rougher from here to the top.

6.0 Gated roadbed to the right; stay left on the ORV trail.

6.2 Stream crossing. Several streams cross along this section, and some share the road.

6.4 Stream crossing.

6.7 Trail goes through an old gate, with a closed roadbed to the right; stay straight on the ORV trail.

7.7 Trail passes through a Forest Service gate; continue straight on the roadbed.

7.8 Roadbed intersects gravel FR 68; go left on FR 68, which is open to traffic.

7.9 Intersection with gravel FR 49. Go left on FR 49, following the signs to Windy Gap.

8.3 Rest area with restrooms on the right, parking area on the left. Continue straight on FR 49.

8.5 Roadbed enters from the right; stay on FR 49.

8.6 Upper trailhead for Windy Gap Cycle Trail on the left; the road is gated ahead. Turn left onto the singletrack. The most difficult technical section begins here.

8.7 Stream crossing.

9.1 Great views of Fort Mountain and the valley below (if you can take your eyes off the trail long enough to look).

9.3 Stream crossing.

10.5 Trail turns sharp left and goes downhill. Another trail continues straight; go left.

10.6 Trail widens into more of a doubletrack.

11.0 Trail enters from right rear; stay straight on Windy Gap Trail.

11.6 Milma Creek ORV Trail enters from the left; go straight on Windy Gap Trail.

12.6 Roadbed enters from the left; stay on Windy Gap Trail.

12.7 Unmarked trail enters from the left; stay on Windy Gap Trail.

12.9 Ride ends at lower trailhead.

Fort Mountain State Park (Chatsworth Area)

Fort Mountain State Park is the latest Georgia state park to add mountain bike trails. As a matter of fact, the trails weren't quite completed when I mapped them. A hellish, rocky 1.5-mile push through stinging nettles (in bike shorts, naturally), and a magnificent case of poison ivy will be some of the not so fond memories I have of this section. Luckily, those conditions will be improved by the time you read this.

Fort Mountain is named for the 800-foot-long ruins of an ancient stone wall along the mountain's northern edge. The origins of the wall and its purpose remain a mystery. Theories range from the wall being built by Hernando DeSoto during his exploration of the area in the fifteenth century, to the wall being built and used as a ceremonial structure by Native Americans, to a Civil War engineering company with nothing better to do.

During one of the workdays on the construction of the trails on the lower slopes of the mountain, we got an impromptu tour of more stone ruins, resembling a building foundation and what appeared to be a stone encirclement or a corral. We heard some interesting background on the possible origins of the structures. The mountain was also mined extensively, and with our knowledgeable guides, we got quite a lesson on how the many uses of the mountain have shaped its sides.

Park Rangers Wally Wood and Brian Ensley.

The East-West Loop passes by an old mineshaft or two, tin mining shacks, and an ore chute. The upper, steeper section of trail actually runs through an open ore cut, with a vertical drop to each side to mark the site and keep your attention. Most of the trails are laid out on old mining roadbeds.

Two of the rides go down the side of the mountain, spend some time along the lower slopes, then climb none too gently back up to the top. The other two rides stay on top of the mountain, and offer easier options for those hotter days. All of the trails are laid out in loop configurations.

The park offers 16 cottages, primitive pioneer camping for groups, a lake and sand beach, and campsites with water, power, and comfort stations with showers.

The park makes a great destination for a weekend of riding, with four excellent trails in the park, and is a great starting point for exploring the other trails located in the Chatsworth area. Just a couple miles past the entrance to the park is the Tatum Lead ride, which you can also connect with the Rock Creek Loop (Tatum Lead and Rock Creek are on national forest land).

Though one of the newer trail systems in the area, the park's central location and excellent scenery will make it a favorite destination. Just remember to make reservations early.

East-West Loop

Location:	8 miles east of Chatsworth, about 2 hours north of Atlanta.
Distance:	13 miles.
Time:	3 hours.
Tread:	9.7 miles on singletrack, most on old roadbeds, and 3.3 miles on gravel roadbed.
Aerobic level:	Strenuous.
Technical difficulty:	4.5.
Highlights:	Great overlooks, challenging downhill, old mines, killer climb.
Land status:	The trail lies within Fort Mountain State Park.
Maps:	USGS Ramhurst and Crandall.
Access:	From Atlanta, go north on Interstate 75 to Exit 126 for U.S. Highway 411. Go north on US 411 to Chatsworth and turn right onto Georgia Highway 52 east for 8 miles. The entrance to Fort Mountain State

Park is on the left. Turn left; once inside the park, go past the office and left at the fork. The parking lot for the mountain bike trails is on the left about 0.75 mile up the hill.

Notes on the trail: The East-West Loop is the longest of the loop trails at Fort Mountain State Park. The trail uses part of the Gold Mine Loop on top of the mountain, before plunging you down a very steep, open powerline cut for some distance. The views are some of the best in the state, although you may be paying such close attention to the trail during the descent you won't have time to look ahead.

Once you get past the steep sections, the trail joins some old mining roadbeds, passing an open mine, an ore chute, and some abandoned mining equipment along the way. After a couple of creek crossings and a leisurely roll along the lower sections of the mountain on a gravel roadbed, you turn and begin the tough return climb that challenges even the strongest riders.

The parking area is just a couple of easy miles of trail past the steep part of the climb, with a creek along the way to keep you company, and the knowledge of the beach and the lake to spur you on.

Don't let the distance fool you—the difficulty of the descent and return climb make this one heckuva ride!

Restrictions: All visitors to Georgia state parks must purchase a $2 daily park pass for their vehicle. There is also a $2 day fee to ride the trails. You can pay the fees and pick up the rider pass at the park office, just to the right as you enter the park. Annual passes are available.

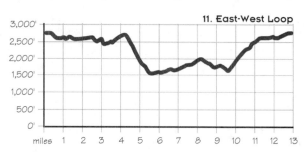

11. East-West Loop

THE RIDE

0.0 The trailhead is just across the paved road from the parking lot entrance, beside a utility pole. The first section of the trail is two-way.

0.4 Trail forks; go left.

1.0 Trail intersection; go straight across.

1.2 Trail intersection; go right, up the hill. The two-way section ends here.

1.3 Trail intersects with paved park road; across the road and 20 yards left the trail re-enters the woods.

2.2 Trail intersects a hiking trail; go straight across.

2.4 Views to the left.

2.9 Short steep downhill section; the large cut just ahead is an old gold mine ruin.

East-West Loop

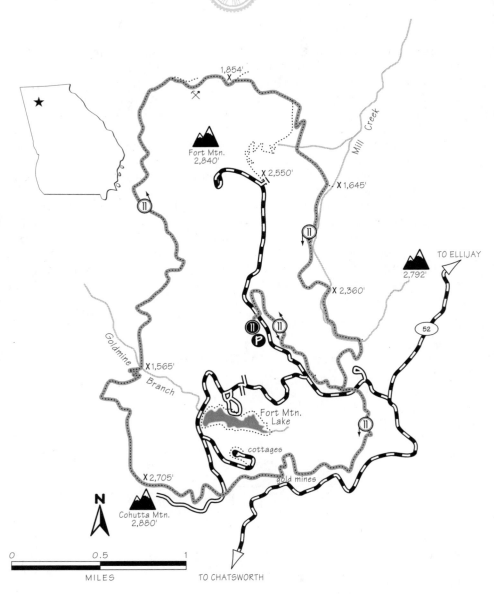

1,854'
X

Fort Mtn.
2,840'

X 2,550'

X 1,645'

Mill Creek

TO ELLIJAY

2,792'

X 2,360'

52

Goldmine

X 1,565'

Branch

Fort Mtn.
Lake

cottages

gold mines

X 2,705'

N

Cohutta Mtn.
2,880'

0   0.5   1

MILES

TO CHATSWORTH

3.2 Views to the left.

3.4 Wildlife opening to the left; the trail turns to doubletrack just past the opening.

3.6 Trail intersects the semipaved Pioneer Camp Road. Go straight across.

4.1 Trail crosses small powerline cut.

4.2 Trail enters a large powerline cut. A television tower and parking lot is up to the left; turn right and ride along the powerline cut. The trail will cross and follow the powerline cut down the mountain for the next 0.8 mile, eventually joining some old mining roadbeds. Hang on! (Uphill to the left is the last bailout before the descent.)

4.8 Trail crosses an old open mine. Tin shack ruins to the left.

4.9 Trail intersects from the right; turn sharp left to another T intersection by the poweline cut; turn right along the powerline cut. Another trail enters just as you turn right; stay on the roadbed on the powerline cut.

5.0 Roadbed continues straight ahead; turn sharp right at a switchback onto another roadbed.

5.1 Trail joins another roadbed; go straight.

5.2 Roadbed continues straight, trail turns left, downhill; go left. Just ahead the trail passes through another mine cut, then follows a series of switchbacks downhill.

5.4 Pass an old tin mine shack.

5.5 Turn sharp right onto another roadbed.

5.6 Creek crossing.

5.7 Creek crossing.

6.0 Trail intersects from the left; go right. Trail intersects from the right; go straight.

6.2 Roadbed forks; go left.

6.3 Roadbed forks; go left.

6.5 Roadbed rejoins the powerline cut.

6.6 Roadbed enters from the right; go straight.

6.7 Roadbed widens into an old gravel road. A roadbed enters from the right; go straight.

6.8 Roadbed forks; go right.

7.1 Roadbed enters from the left rear; go straight.

7.2 ATV trail enters from the left; stay on the main roadbed.

7.8 Roadbed forks; go right, up the hill.

7.9 Roadbed forks; go right.

8.0 Old ore chute to the left. Just ahead to the right is a large mineshaft. There is abandoned mining machinery along both sides of the roadbed.

8.1 Pass through an old gate.

8.2 Roadbed enters from the right rear; go straight.

8.5 View to the left.

8.7 Roadbed forks to the right; go right. Just ahead the trail will join the Cool Springs Loop through some switchbacks and down to a gravel road.

9.4 Roadbed joins a gravel road; bear right on the gravel road.

9.7 Trail turns right off the gravel roadbed; turn right, up the hill, paralleling a creek. The next 1.5 miles are tough!

10.0 Steep, rocky section begins.

10.7 Roadbed enters from the right rear; stay straight on the main trail.

10.9 Trail turns left and crosses the creek, then continues on the other side.

11.0 Trail intersects a singletrack; go left. Do not cross the creek. (Share the trail with hikers for a short distance; be courteous!)

11.1 Trail intersection; the singletrack continues straight ahead. Turn right and cross the creek, where the bike trail continues.

11.7 Trail intersection; to the left is where you went on the first section of the ride; turn right. This section is two-way trail.

12.9 Trail intersection; the Gold Mine Loop enters here. Go straight across.

12.2 Trail enters from the left rear; go straight.

12.4 Trail enters from the left rear; go straight.

12.9 Trail ends at a paved park road; the parking lot is just across the road.

13.0 Ride ends at the parking lot.

Cool Springs Loop

Location:	8 miles east of Chatsworth, about 2 hours north of Atlanta.
Distance:	7 miles.
Time:	2 hours.
Tread:	1 mile on paved road, 0.8 mile on gravel roadbed, and 5.2 miles on singletrack, some on old roadbeds.
Aerobic level:	Moderately strenuous.
Technical difficulty:	3.
Highlights:	Overlooks, cool downhill, tongue-dragging uphill, waterfalls, bears.
Land status:	The trail lies within Fort Mountain State Park.
Maps:	USGS Crandall.
Access:	From Atlanta, go north on Interstate 75 to Exit 126 for U.S. Highway 411. Go north on US 411 to Chatsworth and turn right onto Georgia Highway 52 east for 8 miles. The entrance to Fort Mountain State Park is on the left. Once inside the park, go past the office and left at the fork. The parking lot for mountain bikers is on the left about 0.5 mile up the hill.

Notes on the trail: From the parking lot on top of the mountain, pedal along a paved park road about 1 mile to the trailhead, near an overlook that's worth a pause. It's real downhill from here, as the next mile drops you down about 800 vertical feet along a series of switchbacks on an old logging roadbed to the lower elevations of the mountain. Once down, you'll follow a gravel road-bed for a short distance, with much to see along the way.

Cool Springs Loop

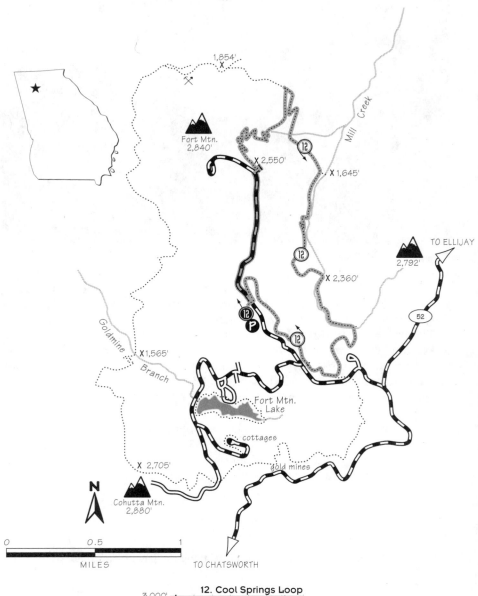

1,854'
X

Fort Mtn.
2,840'

X 2,550'

X 1,645'

Mill Creek

12

12

2,792'

TO ELLIJAY

X 2,360'

12
P

52

12

Fort Mtn.
Lake

Goldmine Branch

X 1,565'

cottages

gold mines

X 2,705'

N

Cohutta Mtn.
2,880'

0   0.5   1

MILES

TO CHATSWORTH

12. Cool Springs Loop

3,000'
2,500'
2,000'
1,500'
1,000'
500'
0'

miles 1 2 3 4 5 6 7

Cool Springs Overlook.

This is the only trail I've ever seen bears on, and I saw two on the inaugural ride! Enjoy the sights and rest up, because the ensuing climb back up the mountain is not for the weak of heart (or leg).

The trail gains back almost a thousand vertical feet in just over 1.4 miles of the toughest, prettiest climb I've had the displeasure of panting up. As you progress, the creek gets closer to the trail and keeps you company, until you reach the two-way return section. From there, it's a couple of easy miles back to the parking area.

Restrictions: All visitors to Georgia state parks must purchase a $2 daily park pass for their vehicle. There is also a $2 day fee to ride the trails. You can pay the fees and pick up the rider pass at the park office, just to the right as you enter the park. Annual passes are available.

THE RIDE

0.0 From the parking lot, turn left and ride along the paved park road, passing the first trailhead just across from the parking lot.

1.0 Turn right into the Cool Springs Overlook parking area; the trailhead is to the left just as you turn into the parking lot. Turn left onto the trailhead. (If you want to see where you're going, walk out to the overlook platform and look down!)

1.1 Trail intersection; go straight across. The trail joins an old logging roadbed.

1.2 Sharp switchback right. The trail then follows an old roadbed along a series of switchbacks down the mountainside.

2.4 Roadbed enters from the left rear; go straight. You will go through some more switchbacks, and the East-West Loop (Ride 11) enters from the left.

3.4 Roadbed joins a gravel road; bear right.

3.7 Trail turns right off the gravel roadbed; turn right. Here comes the fun!

4.0 Steep, rocky section begins.

4.7 Roadbed enters from the right rear; stay straight on the main trail.

4.9 Trail turns left and crosses the creek, then continues on the other side.

5.0 Trail intersects a singletrack; go left. Do not cross the creek. (The bike trail shares a hiking trail for a short distance; be courteous!)

5.1 Trail intersection. The singletrack continues straight ahead; turn right and cross the creek, where the bike trail continues.

5.7 Trail intersection; turn right. This section is a two-way trail.

5.9 Trail intersection; go straight across.

6.2 Trail enters from the left rear; go straight.

6.4 Trail enters from the left rear; go straight.

6.9 Trail ends at a paved park road; the parking lot is just across the road.

7.0 Ride ends at the parking lot.

Gold Mine Loop

Location:	8 miles east of Chatsworth, about 2 hours north of Atlanta.
Distance:	6.4 miles.
Time:	1.5 hours.
Tread:	1.6 miles on paved park road, and 4.8 miles on singletrack, some on old roadbeds.
Aerobic level:	Moderately easy.
Technical difficulty:	2.5.
Highlights:	Overlooks, sweet open singletrack, old gold mines, more overlooks, lake on the return route.
Land status:	The trail lies within Fort Mountain State Park.
Maps:	USGS Crandall.
Access:	From Atlanta, go north on Interstate 75 to Exit 126 for U.S. Highway 411. Go north on US 411 to Chatsworth and turn right onto Georgia Highway 52 east for 8 miles. The entrance to Fort Mountain State Park is on the left. Once inside the park, go past the office and left at the fork. The parking lot for the mountain bike trails is on the left about 0.75 mile up the hill.

Gold Mine Loop •
The Lake Loop

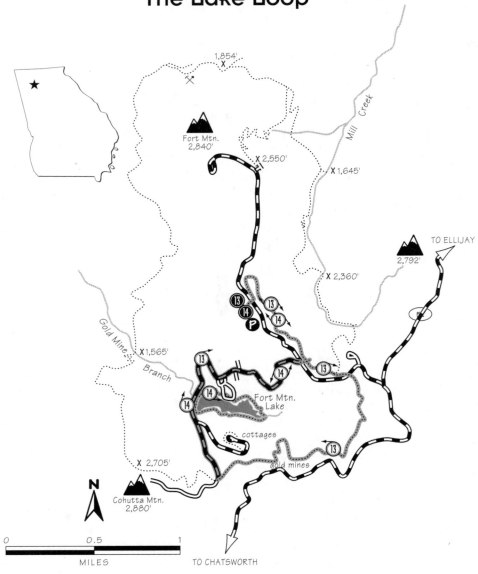

1,854'
X

Fort Mtn.
2,840'

X 2,550'

X 1,645'

Mill Creek

TO ELLIJAY
2,792'

X 2,360'

13
14
P
13
14

Gold Mine

X 1,565'

Branch

13

14
13

14
14

Fort Mtn.
Lake

cottages

13

X 2,705'

gold mines

N

Cohutta Mtn.
2,880'

0   0.5   1
MILES

TO CHATSWORTH

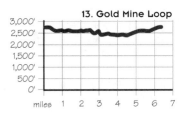

13. Gold Mine Loop

3,000'
2,500'
2,000'
1,500'
1,000'
500'
0'

miles 1 2 3 4 5 6 7

Notes on the trail: If you want to enjoy the trails at Fort Mountain State Park but don't want to experience the tougher climbs and descents, here's your option—great views and less pain!

The Gold Mine Loop shares some of the easier upper sections of the East-West Loop, but stays on top of the mountain for the entire ride. Except for a stretch of paved park road, the trail is all singletrack laid in on old roadbeds. There are several views from the southern heights, then you join the paved road as you pass the lake and campgrounds. (If you want more distance, add the 1.1-mile Lake Loop to your route. It starts just as you join the main paved park road.) After a climb on the paved park road, it's back on the trail for the return to the parking lot.

The loop gets its name from the open gold mines that lie along one section of the trail. You'll know when you get there: if you don't stop, you'll end up in one! The remains of the mines are some open cuts and steep banks.

Restrictions: All visitors to Georgia state parks must purchase a $2 daily park pass for their vehicle. There is also a $2 day fee to ride the trails. You can pay the fees and pick up the rider pass at the park office, just to the right as you enter the park. Annual passes are available.

THE RIDE

0.0 The trailhead is just across the paved road from the parking lot entrance, beside a utility pole. The first section of the trail is two-way.

0.4 Trail forks; go left.

1.0 Trail intersection; go straight across.

1.2 Trail intersection; go right, up the hill. The two-way section ends here.

1.3 Trail intersects with a paved park road; across the road and 20 yards left the trail re-enters the woods.

2.2 Trail intersects a hiking trail; go straight across.

2.4 Views to the left.

2.9 Short, steep downhill section; the large cut just ahead is an old gold mine ruin.

3.2 Views to the left.

3.4 Wildlife opening to the left; the trail turns to doubletrack just past the opening.

3.6 Trail intersects the semipaved Pioneer Camp Road. Turn right on the paved road.

3.9 Trail intersects a paved park road; turn left on the park road.

4.0 Nature trail entrance to the left; stay on the paved park road, across the dam.

4.4 Pass the beach and picnic parking areas to the right.

4.5 Pass campground entrances to the left and right.

5.2 Intersection with another paved park road; just across the road and to the right from the intersection is a trailhead; go across and back into the woods on the trail.

5.3 Trail intersection; turn left. The trail ahead is closed to bikes. The Cool Springs and East-West loops enter from the right. The trail to the left is two-way.

5.6 Trail enters from the left rear; go straight.

5.8 Trail enters from the left rear; go straight.

6.3 Trail ends at the paved park road; the parking lot is just across the road.

6.4 Ride ends at the parking lot.

The Lake Loop

See Map
on Page 52

Location: 8 miles east of Chatsworth, about 2 hours north of Atlanta.

Distance: 5.9 miles.

Time: 1.5 hours.

Tread: 3.3 miles on wide singletrack trail, and 2.6 miles on paved park road.

Aerobic level: Easy.

Technical difficulty: 1.5.

Highlights: Shorter, easier loop on top of the mountain, virtually flat section around the lake and beach area, plenty of easy rest stops.

Land status: The trail lies within Fort Mountain State Park.

Maps: USGS Crandall.

Access: From Atlanta, go north on Interstate 75 to Exit 126 for U.S. Highway 411. Go north on US 411 to Chatsworth and turn right onto Georgia Highway 52 east for 8 miles. The entrance to Fort Mountain State Park is on the left. Once inside the park, go past the office and left at the fork, following the directions to the cabins. Just after you cross the dam on the paved road is a parking area to the left. The trail starts and ends here.

Notes on the trail: The lake section of this ride is about the only trail around these parts that you could call flat! The trail uses the two-way connector trail and paved park roads to connect with a multi-use trail that winds around the shores of the lake, passing next to the beach area and through a parking lot.

If you need to introduce someone to dirt, this is a good trail. The return climb will get your heart rate up, but it's on a smooth, paved park road, so it's a little easier. The section of trail along the lake is a multi-use trail—you will encounter folks fishing, rowing boats, nature-watching, or just strolling

The Lake Loop.

along. The bottom line is that you will encounter folks. This trail is a good place to practice yielding the trail and being courteous to others. The gentle grades of the trail surface make it a great training ground for young riders as well.

Remember the park speed limit as you ride down toward the campground and lake. It's easy to exceed 10 miles per hour even on a bike, and the park management is pretty serious about enforcement. (You'll appreciate the speed limit as you make the return climb on this section.) The Lake Loop will give you a good idea of what you can expect on the Gold Mine Loop, so if you're feeling good after this one, take another ride! It's also easy to spend lots of time just enjoying the lake and the surroundings.

Restrictions: All visitors to Georgia state parks must purchase a $2 daily park pass for their vehicle. There is also a $2 day fee to ride the trails. You can pay the fees and pick up the rider pass at the park office, just to the right as you enter the park. Annual passes are available.

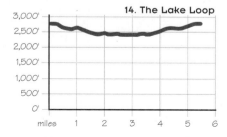

Hill climbing on The Lake Loop.

0.0 The trailhead is just across the paved road from the parking lot entrance, beside a utility pole. The first section of the trail is two-way. Just after you enter the woods, a trail forks right; go left. The lake section of the trail is blazed blue.

0.4 Trail forks; go left.

1.0 Trail intersection; turn right, up the hill.

1.1 The trail ends at the paved park road. Turn right at the paved park road; then immediately turn left at the fork, following the signs toward the campground and cottages. (Remember, the park speed limit on all paved roads is just 10 miles per hour!)

1.8 Pass the campground entrances to the left and right.

1.9 Pass the beach and picnic area parking lot to the left.

2.3 Cross the dam on the paved park road. Just across the dam is a parking area to the left. Turn left into the parking area. The Lake Loop starts just ahead, down by the lake. Go left on the trail, back toward the dam. (The trail is always run clockwise, unless posted otherwise.)

2.4 Cross the dam, parallel to the road.

2.6 Trail leaves the lakeshore and goes left, past the miniature golf course, to the parking lot. Turn right in the parking lot, go down past the beach, and the trail starts again just ahead as the paved drive turns left.

2.8 Campground to the left.

2.9 Trail intersects from the left; go straight.

3.0 Just past a bridge, a trail intersects from the left rear; go straight.

3.4 Turn left back into the paved parking area, then turn right onto the paved park road.

3.5 Cross the dam on the paved park road.

3.9 Pass the beach and picnic area parking lot to the right.

4.0 Pass the campground entrances to the left and right.

4.7 Intersection with another paved park road. Just across the road and to the right from the intersection is a trailhead; go across and back into the woods on the trail.

4.8 Trail intersection; turn left. The trail ahead is closed to bikes. The Cool Springs and East-West loops enter from the right. The trail to the left is two-way.

5.1 Trail enters from the left rear; go straight.

5.3 Trail enters from the left rear; go straight.

5.8 Trail ends at the paved park road; the parking lot is just across the road.

5.9 Ride ends at the parking lot.

Tatum Lead Road

Location:	About 11 miles east of Chatsworth, about 1.5 hours north of Atlanta.
Distance:	15.2 miles out and back.
Time:	2.5 hours.
Tread:	15.2 miles on doubletrack and jeep road.
Aerobic level:	Moderately easy.
Technical difficulty:	2.
Highlights:	Excellent views for almost the entire ride; great fall colors; downhills at either end.
Land status:	The trail lies within or borders the Chattahoochee-Oconee National Forest, Cohutta District.
Maps:	USGS Crandall and Ramhurst.
Access:	From Atlanta, go north on Interstate 75 to Exit 126 for U.S. Highway 411. Go north on US 411 to Chatsworth and turn right onto Georgia Highway 52 east for 10.3 miles. Look for a sign on the right at a gravel road; this is the Tatum Lead Road. There is a parking area just as you leave GA 52.

Notes on the trail: Tatum Lead Road is an old forest road that runs along the top of Tatum Mountain. With minor downhills at either end, most of the ride is along the ridgelines, with some great views to either side. The fall colors are incredible, and the elevation makes for cool riding most of the year.

You will probably encounter ATVs and ORVs as you travel the trail; the entire road is open to motorized traffic all the way to the private property at the far end. The turnaround point is a big berm across the road, and it is well marked.

The Rock Creek ATV Trail intersects with this trail at two points. A good alternative is to park at the trailhead for Rock Creek Trail at the bottom of the mountain, and ride up to Tatum Lead, along the length of Tatum Lead, then back down the other side of Rock Creek Trail.

Due to the use of the road by four-wheel-drive vehicles, the roadbed is kept relatively clear of obstacles. This ride is a good way to spend a long day talking with riding partners.

Tatum Lead Road

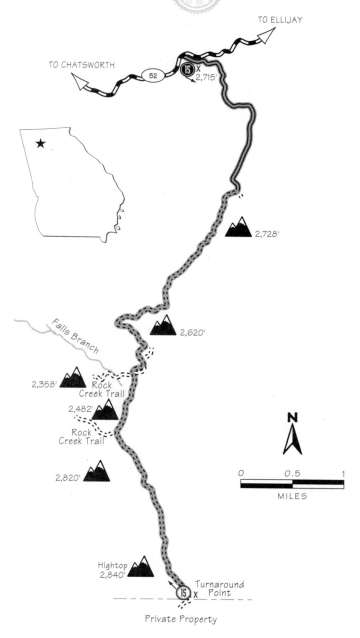

TO ELLIJAY

TO CHATSWORTH

52

15 X
2,715'

2,728'

Falls Branch

2,620'

2,358'
Rock
Creek Trail

2,482'

Rock
Creek Trail

2,820'

N

0   0.5   1

MILES

Hightop
2,840'

Turnaround
Point
15 X

Private Property

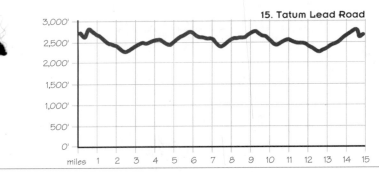

15. Tatum Lead Road

THE RIDE

0.0 From the parking area, continue along the gravel road. The first section of Tatum Lead Road is a right-of-way across private land. You will pass several private residences. Stay on the gravel road!

0.5 Roadbed enters from the right; stay on the main road.

0.8 Roadbeds intersect from the left and right; stay on the main road.

1.8 Roadbed forks to the left; go right, slightly downhill.

2.0 Roadbed enters national forest. Just beyond this, a roadbed enters from the left; stay straight on the main roadbed.

2.7 Roadbed enters from the left; go straight on the main roadbed.

3.3 Trail enters from the right; stay on the main roadbed.

4.0 Roadbed enters from the left; stay straight on the main roadbed.

4.9 Roadbeds enter from the left and right; stay straight on the main roadbed.

5.0 Rock Creek Trail intersects from the right; stay straight on the main roadbed.

5.4 Trail enters from the right; stay on the main roadbed.

5.7 Second fork of Rock Creek Trail intersects from the right; stay on the main roadbed.

5.9 Trail enters from the right; stay on the main roadbed.

7.0 Trail enters from the right; stay on the main roadbed.

7.5 Turnaround point at a large dirt berm. The road is private property and closed beyond this point.

8.0 Trail enters from the left; stay on the main roadbed.

9.1 Trail enters from the left; stay on the main roadbed.

9.3 Rock Creek Trail enters from the left; stay straight on the main roadbed.

9.6 Trail enters from the left; stay on the main roadbed.

10.0 Second fork of Rock Creek Trail intersects from the left; stay straight on the main roadbed.

10.2 Roadbeds enter from the left and right; stay straight on the main roadbed.

11.1 Roadbed enters from the right; stay on the main roadbed.

11.8 Trail enters from the left; stay on the main roadbed.

13.4 Roadbed enters from the right; stay on the main roadbed.

13.0 Roadbed enters from the right; stay on the main roadbed. Just beyond this, the roadbed leaves the national forest.

13.2 Roadbed enters from the right rear; stay on the main roadbed.

14.2 Roads enter from the left and right; stay straight on the main road.

14.6 Road enters from the left; stay straight on the main road.

15.2 Ride ends at the parking area at GA 52.

Rock Creek Loop

Location:	About 8 miles east of Chatsworth, about 2 hours north of Atlanta.
Distance:	5.5 miles.
Time:	1.5 hours.
Tread:	5.5 miles on ATV and ORV trail, most on old doubletrack.
Aerobic level:	Moderately strenuous.
Technical difficulty:	3.5.
Highlights:	Waterfalls, ORV-made banked turns and curves, views from the top, second half is downhill.
Land status:	The trail is located in the Chattahoochee-Oconee National Forest, Cohutta District.
Maps:	USGS Crandall.
Access:	From Atlanta, go north on Interstate 75 to Exit 126 for U.S. Highway 411. Go north on US 411 to Chatsworth, turn right on Georgia Highway 52, and go 1 mile. Turn right onto Old Federal Road and drive 4 miles. Turn left onto gravel Forest Road 3 at the Peeples Lake/Rock Creek Trail sign. Follow FR 3 about 5.9 miles to the trailhead.

Notes on the trail: This ride takes you along an ATV trail that climbs up the mountain, then joins the Tatum Lead Road running along the ridgelines for a short distance. The views from the top are good enough for a rest stop. The doubletrack on top is open to four-wheel-drive vehicles as well as ATVs, so watch for oncoming traffic.

Turn left at the next intersection of the ATV trail, and it will take you back down the mountain in a much quicker fashion than you climbed it. This section of the trail is why they invented suspension! The downhill from Tatum Lead Road back to the fork is a great testing ground for wheels, brakes, and suspension components. A couple of roaring waterfalls off to the right are worth stopping for, if you can.

The bottom section from the fork to the parking lot is full of banked turns just made to rail around. It's all over too soon as you return to the parking lot.

If you're feeling your oats, ride the trail in the opposite direction and trade a brutal rocky climb for a longer downhill.

Rock Creek Loop

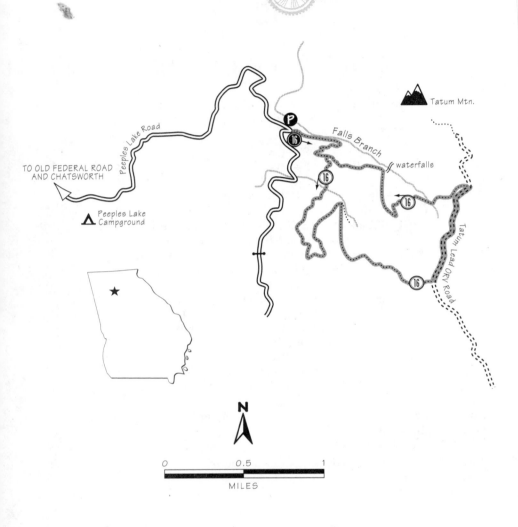

Tatum Mtn.

Falls Branch

waterfalls

Tatum Lead ORV Road

P

TO OLD FEDERAL ROAD
AND CHATSWORTH

Peeples Lake Road

Peeples Lake
Campground

N

0   0.5   1

MILES

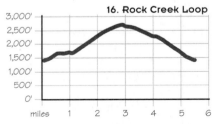

16. Rock Creek Loop

3,000'
2,500'
2,000'
1,500'
1,000'
500'
0'

miles   1   2   3   4   5   6

Nice doubletrack on Fort Mountain.

THE RIDE

0.0 From the parking area at the trailhead, follow the trail uphill along the creek.

0.5 Trail forks; go right.

0.7 Stream crossing.

0.8 Stream crossing.

1.3 Stream crossing.

1.5 Stream crossing.

1.8 Trail takes a sharp right turn, another trail goes straight. Turn right, up the hill.

2.2 Roadbed enters from the right; go straight.

2.3 Trail enters from the right; go straight.

2.9 Trail intersects with Tatum Lead Road (doubletrack). Turn left on Tatum Lead Road.

3.2 Trail enters from the left; stay straight.

3.6 Rock Creek ATV Trail enters from the left; turn left on Rock Creek Trail.

4.3 Creek crossing. The trail deteriorates from here; you'll appreciate suspension.

4.5 Waterfall to the right.

4.6 Bigger waterfall to the right.

5.0 Trail forks; go right, down the hill.

5.5 Ride ends at the parking lot.

Ellijay

Just south and east of the Cohutta District and Fort Mountain lies Ellijay, Georgia. The town's central location along Georgia Highway 52 makes it a great meeting place for rides in the area, and a good reference point for finding your way around.

The town boasts its own bike shop, Cartecay River Bikes, and its own SORBA chapter, known locally as the Ellijay Mountain Bike Association. The EMBA is responsible for most of the maintenance of the trails described here. You can usually get current info on their latest project at the bike shop.

Local outfitters can provide lots of other outdoor recreational options like whitewater rafting and fishing, and the town hosts several annual festivals.

Mountaintown Outdoor Expeditions, just east of town near the Red & White and River loops, has one of the very few dual slalom courses in the state. Watching the races held there several times a year is a great way to top off a day's riding. Owner Jay Srymanske is one of the original promoters of the sport, since before folks around here even knew what a mountain bike was. He continues to support the state points series, and hosts cross-country and dual slalom races throughout the year. You can still feel the original spirit that used to define mountain biking at one of Jay's events.

If you are able to spend some time in the area, offer to help the EMBA do some trail maintenance. In return, you may hook up with some locals who can show you even more fantastic riding that didn't make it into this guide for various reasons. (The locals guard their favorite spots jealously—you have to earn a guided tour.) See Appendix A for contact information.

There are several lodging options from relatively inexpensive motels to bed-and-breakfasts with all of the trimmings. The fall foliage season is a busy one, so if you're planning a trip then and need lodging, make sure to reserve early.

The town's proximity to Atlanta makes doing the local rides a good day trip as well. If my truck had auto-pilot, Ellijay would be one of the settings!

Ridgeway Bike Trail

Location:	About 10 miles west of Ellijay, 2 hours north of Atlanta.
Distance:	5.6 miles.
Time:	1.25 hours.
Tread:	5.6 miles on singletrack, some on old roadbeds.
Aerobic level:	Moderate.
Technical difficulty:	3.5.
Highlights:	Overlooks Carter's Lake in several places; lots of ups and downs.
Land status:	The trail is in the Ridgeway Recreation Area, administered by the U.S. Army Corps of Engineers.
Maps:	USGS Webb.
Access:	From Atlanta, go north on Interstate 75 to I-575. Stay on I-575; it will turn into Georgia Highway 515. Go north to the traffic light in front of the Hardee's in East Ellijay. Turn left on GA 76/382, then left again just before the bridge. Follow GA 76/382 for 8.6 miles to Paw Paw's store on the left. Turn left at the store and follow the road for 3.1 miles to an intersection, where you will turn right and go 0.6 mile to the boat ramp parking lot. The trail starts and ends here.

Notes on the trail: The Ridgeway Recreation Area is located on a peninsula partially surrounded by Carter's Lake. The trail twists and winds through the woods and along the shore in several areas, giving you some nice views of the lake for your rest stops.

And there may be a few of those rest stops. This is a trail with enough ups and downs to accumulate almost a thousand feet of climbing per lap. There are no long climbs, but some of the short ones feel like you're riding up a wall. The ensuing downhills are just as fun. The trail takes some attention to complete. Some areas are rocky and technical, others are smooth as butter.

This loop is an annual favorite among local racers. The option of riding down the boat ramp and into the lake after a hot lap or two makes it even more inviting.

Ridgeway Bike Trail

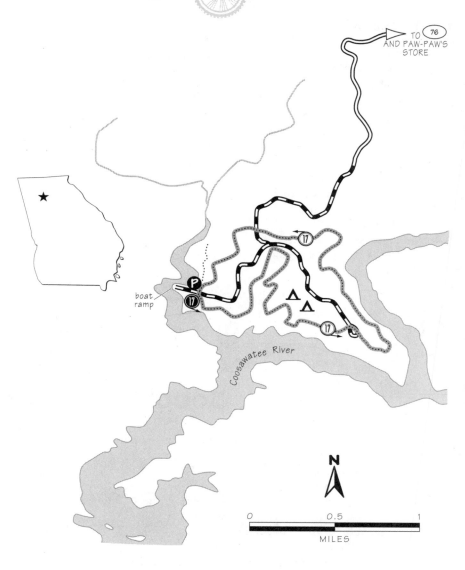

TO 76 AND PAW-PAW'S STORE

boat ramp

Coosawatee River

N

0   0.5   1
MILES

17. Ridgeway Bike Trail

2,500'
2,000'
1,500'
1,000'
500'
0'

miles 1 2 3 4 5

0.0 The trail starts on the side of the parking lot opposite the information board and between the outhouses. The loop is traditionally ridden counterclockwise. The trail is very well marked by orange markers.

0.8 Trail turns sharp right just before the paved road.

2.2 Overlook trail enters from the right; it is 0.1 mile to the overlook

2.4 Creek crossing.

2.6 Pass picnic area.

2.7 Trail enters from the right; stay left.

2.8 Trail goes right at the parking lot; go right.

3.3 Trail intersection; go right.

3.8 Trail forks; go right.

4.2 Trail crosses the paved road.

4.3 Trail enters a clearing.

4.5 Creek crossing.

5.4 Trail intersection; go left.

5.6 Trail ends at the parking lot.

River Loop

Location:	4 miles east of East Ellijay, about 1.5 hours north of Atlanta.
Distance:	3.9 miles.
Time:	1 hour.
Tread:	2.2 miles on singletrack, and 1.7 miles on gated forest road and doubletrack.
Aerobic level:	Moderate.
Technical difficulty:	3.
Highlights:	Great singletrack section along the river, a local favorite race course.
Land status:	The trail is located on property leased by the Georgia Department of Natural Resources and used as a wildlife management area. This is a multi-use trail; please respect the rights of other users.
Maps:	USGS Dyke.
Access:	From Atlanta, follow Interstate 575 north to Georgia Highway 515 north to East Ellijay. At the traffic light at the Hardee's, turn left onto GA 52. Go across the

River Loop •
Red & White Loop

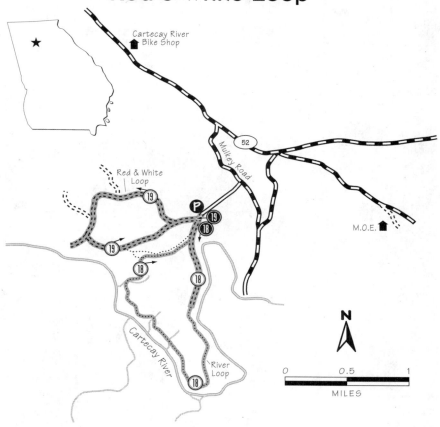

Cartecay River
Bike Shop

52

Mulkey Road

Red & White
Loop

19

P

19

18

19

18

18

18

M.O.E.

Cartecay River

River
Loop

18

N

0   0.5   1

MILES

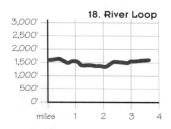

18. River Loop

3,000'
2,500'
2,000'
1,500'
1,000'
500'
0'

miles   1   2   3   4

Negotiating singletrack near Ellijay.

bridge and turn right for 3.8 miles. Turn right on Mulkey Road. Follow Mulkey Road 0.2 mile to a dirt road on your right. There is a sign for the Rich Mountain Wildlife Management Area, Cartecay Tract. Turn right and follow the gravel forest road 0.6 mile to a gravel parking area. The trailhead is further along the road, through a gate.

Notes on the trail: The River Loop is one of the oldest mountain bike trails in northern Georgia. Built with assistance from local riders and the Georgia DNR, the trail utilizes gated forest road, old forest roadbed, and singletrack in a loop configuration. The loop was also one of the first race courses in the state, and is still used as such at least once a year. The middle part of the loop parallels the Cartecay River, with several scenic spots for a dip, or just gazing at the natural beauty of the river. Although relatively close to town and civilization, you can sit by the river and feel like you're miles away from anywhere. And after all, isn't that the mark of a great trail?

The River Loop does just that—it follows a loop along the banks of the Cartecay River. Besides the obvious views from the trail, a short hike at the bottom of the singletrack leads to a huge rock overlooking the river. There are a couple of technical creek crossings along the way, and two short but steep climbs to keep your pulse rate up. The twisty, rooty singletrack before the river is fast and challenging. You can combine this ride with the Red & White Loop for a longer option.

Restrictions: This trail is located within a wildlife management area, and the trails may be closed during scheduled hunt days. Please check the bulletin boards at the trailhead, or call the number listed in Appendix C for information.

THE RIDE

0.0 Go through the gate just below the parking area, and follow the gravel road.
0.2 Gate on the right; this is the start of the Red & White Loop. Stay straight.
0.3 Road forks, go left.
0.5 Clearcut on the right.
0.9 Road enters a clearing; singletrack begins at the far side of the clearing.
1.4 Steep technical descent begins.
1.6 Bottom of the descent; trail to the left is river overlook.
2.2 Creek crossing.
2.6 Creek crossing.
2.7 Creek crossing.
3.1 Trail enters clearcut.
3.2 Trail joins the roadbed.
3.5 Connector trail to Red & White Loop enters from the left.

3.6 Road forks; go left.

3.7 Gated road to the left; stay straight.

3.9 Return to the parking area.

Red & White Loop

See Map
on Page 69

Location:	4 miles east of East Ellijay, about 1.5 hours north of Atlanta.
Distance:	2.6 miles.
Time:	0.75 hour.
Tread:	2.6 miles on gated forest road.
Aerobic level:	Easy.
Technical difficulty:	1.5.
Highlights:	Virtually level, smooth trail surface.
Land status:	The trail is located on property leased by the Georgia DNR and is used as a wildlife management area. It is also a multi-use trail; please respect the rights of other users.
Maps:	USGS Dyke.
Access:	From Atlanta, follow Interstate 575 and Georgia Highway 515 north to East Ellijay. At the traffic light at the Hardee's, turn left on GA 52. Go across the bridge and turn right. Follow GA 52 for 3.8 miles. Turn Right on Mulkey Road, and travel 0.2 mile to a dirt road on your right. At the sign for the Rich Mountain Wildlife Management Area, Cartecay Tract, turn right and follow the gravel forest road 0.6 mile to a gravel parking area. The trailhead is through a gate 0.2 mile on the right, just past the gate past the parking area.

Notes on the trail: The Red & White Loop is a true beginner's loop. Composed entirely of old forest roadbed, the trail wanders in a gradual circle through a forest and field, with just enough elevation change to hint at the challenge of future trails. There are easy options to extend the ride, and just enough challenge to make it fun.

It doesn't get any easier than this in northern Georgia. This is one of the flattest rides I have found in the mountains, and the perfect place for a day trip to gently introduce someone to the sport of mountain biking. The trail features slight grades and undergrowth on one section to give a hint of what it feels like to ride singletrack. The meadow usually has some wildflowers blooming during the warmer months. There is a short out-and-back option down to the river for more adventurous riders, or you can do multiple loops for more distance. The River Loop starts in the same area if this trail is too tame.

Restrictions: This trail is located within a wildlife management area, and the trails are closed during scheduled hunt days. Please check the bulletin boards at the trailhead, or call the information number listed in Appendix C for information.

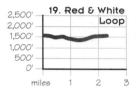

THE RIDE

0.0 From the parking area, proceed through the next gate.
0.2 Gate to the right; turn right.
0.5 Road forks; go right.
1.2 Out-and-back trail to river enters from the right; go left.
1.3 Trail enters a small meadow.
1.5 Trail leaves the meadow and enters the woods.
1.8 River Loop connector trail enters from the right.
2.0 Back at the fork go right to return to the parking area.
2.4 Back to the gate; turn left to the parking area.
2.6 Ride ends at the parking area.

Noontootla

Location:	Approximately 15 miles northwest of Ellijay, about 2 hours from Atlanta.
Distance:	26.2 miles.
Time:	3.5 hours.
Tread:	26.2 miles on gravel forest and county roads.
Aerobic level:	Strenuous.
Technical difficulty:	2.
Highlights:	Good views from the upper sections, fast descents, and moderately easy climbs to 3,000 feet in elevation.
Land status:	The ride is in the Chattahoochee-Oconee National Forest, Toccoa District.

Maps: USGS Noontootla.

Access: From Atlanta, follow Interstate 75 to I-575 north, which becomes Georgia Highway 515. Follow this to East Ellijay. At the traffic light in front of the Hardee's, turn left and cross the bridge. Turn right and follow the signs to GA 52; go about 5.5 miles and turn left on Big Creek Road. Follow the road until it turns to dirt, about 15.3 miles. Continue 0.4 mile farther to Fellowship Baptist Church. The ride starts here.

Notes on the trail: This ride consists entirely of gravel forest and county roads. If you're looking for a good training ride, aren't up to the technical challenges of some of the other rides in the area, or are looking for a good ride when the weather is less than perfect, this one will do nicely.

There are some pretty good views from the higher sections, at or near 3,000 feet, as the forest roads traverse several gaps in quick succession. You'll enjoy some great downhills along the way; just remember that the roads are open to vehicular traffic as you rail that sweeper.

The climbs are moderately tough, and the distance will get your attention if you're not in shape.

Some sections of the ride run along Noontootla Creek, which is yet another great example of a tumbling, noisy North Georgia creek, and enough of a distraction for the slow stretches.

THE RIDE

0.0 From the church, continue east along the gravel road to the first right turn onto Forest Road 58.

0.7 Gravel road to the right; stay straight on FR 58.

1.0 FR 58 parallels Noontootla Creek. Enjoy.

1.5 FR 58E turns to the left; stay straight on FR 58.

1.7 Waterfall to the right.

2.5 FR 58B turns left; stay straight on FR 58.

2.7 Campground to the right by the creek.

3.1 Waterfall to the left.

4.8 FR 58F turns to the right; stay straight on FR 58.

5.2 Unmarked trail to the right; stay straight on FR 58.

5.4 Appalachian Trail crosses here; stay on FR 58.

6.2 Hickory Flats Cemetery sign at FR 251 to the left; stay straight on FR 58.

6.4 Road to the right; stay straight on FR 58.

7.2 Road leaves the creek.

7.8 Trail to the right; stay straight on FR 58.

8.1 Winding Stair Gap. Turn left at the intersection and follow FR 42 along the ridge.

8.6 Roadbed to the left; stay straight on FR 42.

Noontootla

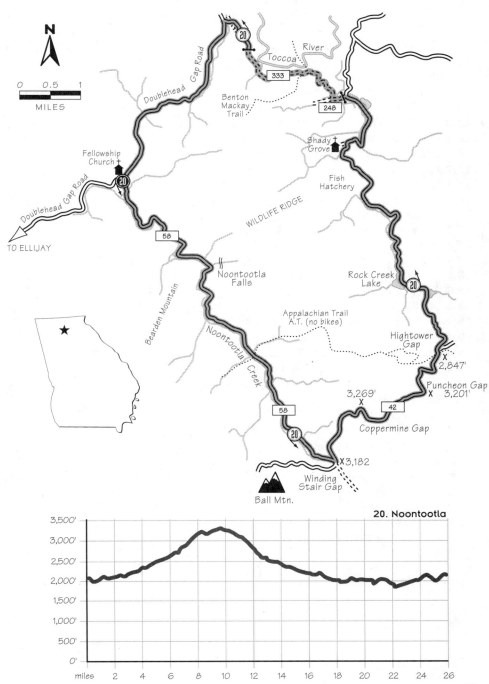

N

0   0.5   1
MILES

Doublehead Gap Road

20

Toccoa River

333

Benton Mackay Trail

248

Shady Grove

Fish Hatchery

Fellowship Church

20

Doublehead Gap Road

TO ELLIJAY

58

WILDLIFE RIDGE

Bearden Mountain

Noontootla Falls

Noontootla Creek

Appalachian Trail A.T. (no bikes)

Rock Creek Lake

20

Hightower Gap

X 2,847'

Puncheon Gap
X 3,201'

3,269'
X

42

Coppermine Gap

58

20

X 3,182

Winding Stair Gap

Ball Mtn.

20. Noontootla

3,500'
3,000'
2,500'
2,000'
1,500'
1,000'
500'
0'

miles   2   4   6   8   10   12   14   16   18   20   22   24   26

8.9 Roadbed to the left; stay straight on FR 42.

9.1 Wildlife opening to the left.

10.5 Roadbed to the left; stay straight on FR 42.

11.8 Hightower Gap. The Appalachian Trail crosses the road here. Don't even think about riding a bike on the AT. Stay to the left at the intersection and follow FR 69 downhill.

12.3 Gravel road to the left; stay straight on FR 69.

12.6 Trail goes to the left; stay on FR 69.

13.0 Pond on the right.

13.2 Road enters from the right; stay straight on FR 69.

13.5 Rock Creek Lake to the left.

14.0 Roadbed to the right; stay straight on FR 69.

14.3 Roadbed to the right; stay straight on FR 69.

15.4 Frank Gross Campground to the right.

15.7 Fish hatchery to the left; bear right and stay on FR 69.

16.1 Roadbed to the right; stay straight on FR 69.

16.7 Shady Grove Baptist Church to the left; FR 69C enters from the right; stay straight on FR 69.

17.7 Roadbed to the right; stay on FR 69.

18.3 Turn left on FR 248 and cross the bridge.

18.4 FR 766 goes left; stay straight on FR 248.

18.5 Road forks; bear right on FR 333.

18.6 Creek crossing.

18.8 Wildlife opening and gravel entry to the left; stay straight on FR 333.

18.9 FR 308 bears right; stay straight on FR 333.

19.4 Benton-MacKaye trail crosses; stay on FR 333.

20.0 Trail to the left; stay on FR 333.

20.2 Trail to the right; stay straight on FR 333.

20.4 Roadbed to the right; stay straight on FR 333.

20.5 Stream crossing.

20.6 Stream crossing.

20.7 Trail to the left; stay straight on FR 333.

21.3 At the fork, bear left on the gravel roadbed.

21.4 Road enters from the left; bear right on the gravel roadbed.

21.5 Gravel drive enters road; stay straight on the gravel road.

21.8 Turn left at the intersection with gravel driveway to the right.

22.1 At the stop sign, turn left onto Doublehead Gap Road.

26.1 FR 58 enters from the left.

26.2 Ride ends at Fellowship Baptist Church.

Blue Ridge

Just a few miles north and west of Ellijay lies the town of Blue Ridge. The excellent South Fork Trail and Loop ride, west of Blue Ridge, is part of the Cohutta Ranger District, and the Aska trails area, just south and east of Blue Ridge, is part of the Toccoa Ranger District. Both are easily accessed from Blue Ridge.

The South Fork Trail and Loop ride is another prime example of a great North Georgia trail, with a little bit of everything. The trails at Aska are older trails that were originally built for hiking and later opened to bike use. Consisting mostly of singletrack in the truest sense of the word, riding some of the trails along the higher elevations takes some concentration. The Stanley Gap Trail is particularly tight on the section near the top of Rocky Mountain, and a little winter snow can make the trail even more challenging. But because most mountain bikers live for singletrack, these trails have become favorites.

The Aska trails all originate from one of two areas, Deep Gap on Aska Road, and Stanley Gap on Stanley Creek Road. The Stanley Gap Trail runs between these two points, so if you have the strength and time, you can connect two or more of the trails into a marathon singletrack fest.

In spite of the predominantly rugged terrain, the area contains one of the few true beginner rides in the state. The Long Branch Loop is actually short, and at 2.3 miles has a lot to offer the novice. Just across the road is the Turkey Farm Loop, which has more distance but runs primarily on gravel Forest Service roads.

Blue Ridge, like nearby Ellijay, is easily accessible from Atlanta for day trips. The area also offers all sorts of lodging and recreation, and makes a great weekend destination or a good multiday stop on your ultimate statewide mountain bike odyssey.

South Fork Trail and Loop

Location:	14 miles west of Blue Ridge, about 1.5 hours north of Atlanta.
Distance:	The trail is 2.9 miles; the loop is 8.1 miles.
Time:	1.5 hours.
Tread:	2.9 miles on singletrack on old logging roadbed and 5.2 miles on gravel forest road.
Aerobic level:	Moderate.
Technical difficulty:	3.
Highlights:	Beautiful waterfalls, excellent singletrack, views, and a long forest road downhill.
Land status:	The trail and loop are located in the Chattahoochee-Oconee National Forest, Cohutta District. This is a multi-use trail; please respect the rights of other users.
Maps:	USGS Dyer.
Access:	From Atlanta, follow Interstate 75 to I-575 north to Blue Ridge. In Blue Ridge, turn left (north) on Georgia Highway 5. Go 3.7 miles to old GA 2, and turn left. After 10.5 miles the road will turn to gravel and you will come to an intersection at Watson Gap. You may park off the road here, or turn left on Forest Road 64 and drive 4 miles to the Jack's River Fields parking area. The trailhead is just off FR 64 before you reach the second parking area. This ride starts at Watson Gap in order to have most of the climbing in the early part of the ride and the singletrack toward the end of the ride (my favorite configuration).

Notes on the trail: This ride has most of the things that make northern Georgia trails so great. Take a camera along for some great photo opportunities.

The ride starts out with a moderate climb along FR 64, rewarding you for your efforts with a great overlook back to the east, from whence you came. The descent that follows is a constant temptation to go way too fast, with some banked turns along the way (remember, the road is open to motorized traffic). At the end of the descent, turn right onto a singletrack trail that follows an old logging roadbed paralleling parts of the south fork of the Jack's River. You'll cross some creeks and streams, and sections of the trail

South Fork Trail and Loop

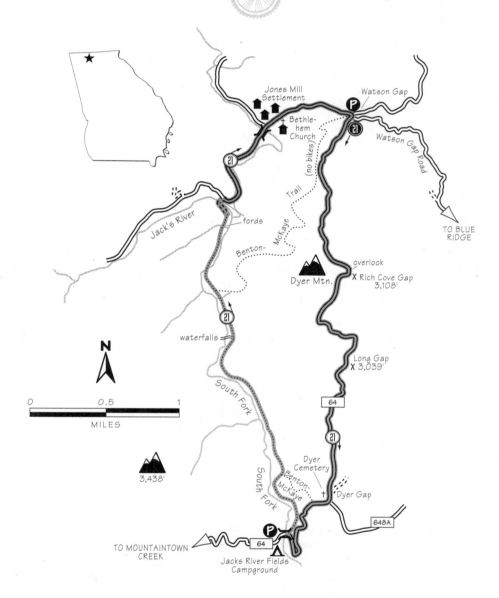

Jones Mill Settlement

Watson Gap

Bethlehem Church

Benton-McKaye Trail (no bikes)

Watson Gap Road

TO BLUE RIDGE

fords

Jack's River

overlook

X Rich Cove Gap 3,108'

Dyer Mtn.

waterfalls

South Fork

Long Gap X 3,039'

64

N

0   0.5   1

MILES

3,438'

Dyer Cemetery

Benton-McKaye

South Fork

† Dyer Gap

648A

TO MOUNTAINTOWN CREEK

64

Jacks River Fields Campground

are rocky and technical. Along the way, the sound of rushing and falling water through the trees beckons you to investigate, and if you do you won't be disappointed. We found some great waterfalls in two separate forays into the woods (off-bike, of course).

Toward the end of the singletrack, you'll experience two awakening (or refreshing, depending on the season) fords across the river. After the second ford, you will rejoin another gravel forest road for the return trip, which is just long enough to dry your shoes and steep enough to warm you up again. All in all, this is a great ride, and well worth the trip.

Restrictions: The Jack's River Fields area is a fee area. The fee is $5 per car per day. If you park at Watson Gap, stop at the day use area and drop a fiver into the collection box for each car anyway, just because you're a conscientious trail user.

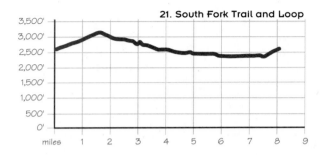

THE RIDE

0.0 From Watson Gap, go left and follow FR 64 uphill.

0.4 Roadbed enters from the right; stay on FR 64.

1.5 Trail enters from the left; stay on FR 64.

2.2 Roadbed enters from the right; stay on FR 64.

2.3 Overlook.

2.8 Roadbed enters from the left; stay on FR 64.

2.9 Gated road on the right; stay on FR 64.

3.1 Dyer Cemetery on the right, gated road to the left; stay on FR 64.

3.3 Benton-MacKaye Trail enters from the right; stay on FR 64.

3.8 Road enters from the left at a sharp right turn; stay right on FR 64.

3.9 Trailhead on the right. Turn right onto singletrack on an old roadbed. (The lower parking lot is just past the trailhead on FR 64, on the left.)

4.0 Stream crossing.

4.1 Stream crossing.

4.2 Hidden waterfalls off to the left.

4.4 Creek crossing.

4.5 Roadbed forks right; trail continues straight to another creek crossing.

5.1 Creek crossing; hidden off to the left is another waterfall.

5.2 Stream crossing.

5.5 Stream crossing.

5.7 Trail enters from the right; bear left.

5.8 Creek crossing.

5.9 Fishing hole to the left (in season).

6.0 Just past a stream crossing, the Benton-MacKaye Trail forks to the right (no bikes); South Fork Trail bears left onto an old roadbed. Go left.

6.2 Ford the Jack's River.

6.4 Roadbed enters from the left rear; continue straight.

6.6 Roadbed enters from the left rear; continue straight.

6.8 Ford the Jack's River again; bear right after the ford. Just ahead, the roadbed joins a forest road; turn right.

7.3 Bethlehem Baptist Church on the right.

7.5 Cross a one-lane bridge; at the intersection go straight.

8.1 Ride ends at Watson Gap.

Green Mountain Trail

Location:	6 miles southeast of Blue Ridge, about 2 hours north of Atlanta.
Distance:	7.7 miles.
Time:	2 hours.
Tread:	7.7 miles on singletrack.
Aerobic level:	Strenuous.
Technical difficulty:	3.5.
Highlights:	Overlook of Blue Ridge Lake, descent to Blue Ridge Lake, cooling off in the lake, long return climb.
Land status:	The trail is in the Chattahoochee-Oconee National Forest, Toccoa District.
Maps:	USGS Blue Ridge.
Access:	From Atlanta, take Interstate 575 and Georgia Highway 515 north to Blue Ridge. From the McDonald's restaurant in Blue Ridge, continue east on GA 515 for 0.8 mile to Windy Ridge Road where you'll turn right. Go about 0.2 mile to the dead end with old U.S. Highway 76 then turn left and go 0.2 mile to Aska Road. Turn right and go south 4.4 miles to the Deep Gap parking lot on your right, just over the crest of a hill. The trail starts from the upper end of the parking lot.

Green Mountain Trail

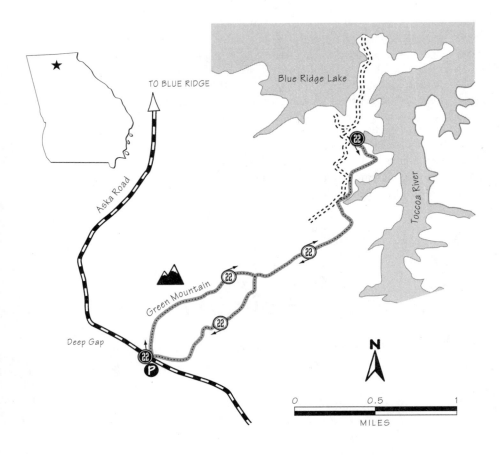

Blue Ridge Lake

TO BLUE RIDGE

Aska Road

Toccoa River

Green Mountain

Deep Gap

N

0   0.5   1
MILES

22. Green Mountain Trail

3,000'
2,500'
2,000'
1,500'
1,000'
500'
0'

miles   1   2   3   4   5   6   7   8

Notes on the trail: Green Mountain Trail used to be combined with Stanley Gap Trail to make up the Rich Mountain Trail, legendary for its toughness and roughness. The USDA Forest Service recognizes them as two separate trails. By tackling them separately, they are manageable for more riders, which is not to say that Green Mountain is easy. The climb back up from the lake is pretty tough, but the scenery along the way will reward you and distract you from any discomfort you may be experiencing.

The initial climb from the parking lot on the upper trail is a toughie as well, but is mercifully over within 0.8 mile. The run down to the lake is a blast, and will keep your pulse up even though you aren't pedaling much. Take a refreshing dip in the lake, or stop and eat lunch, then tackle the return climb. It's not too tough from this direction, and this out-and-back, down-and-up makes a great way to spend the day.

THE RIDE

0.0 The trailhead for the upper trail is just across Aska Road from the parking area, slightly uphill from the entrance. The trail is marked with white blazes. The singletrack starts at the trailhead.

0.3 Trail crosses a roadbed; go straight across.

0.8 Lower Green Mountain Trail enters from the right, on an old roadbed. Follow the trail on the roadbed for a short distance, then the trail forks right off the roadbed.

1.3 Long Branch Loop Trail enters from the right; go straight. You can see Blue Ridge Lake from here.

1.8 Trail briefly joins a roadbed, then forks to the right, off the roadbed.

1.9 Red blazes mark the adjoining private property; stay on the trail.

2.3 Trail joins an old roadbed; go left and follow the blazes.

2.5 Trail forks to the right; creek crossing.

2.55 Double intersection; bear right twice, following the white blazes.

2.6 Trail parallels a gravel road to the left, and the lake to the right.

2.8 Creek crossing.

3.7 Trail ends at lower trailhead at Forest Road 711. You can follow FR 711 out to its end at the lake, about another mile. This ride turns around here.

4.6 Creek crossing.

5.0 Trail forks; to the left is private property. Go right.

6.1 Long Branch Trail connector intersects from the left; go straight.

6.5 Trail joins roadbed; go left and follow the white blazes.

6.6 Intersection of Upper and Lower Green Mountain trails; go left on the roadbed.

7.3 Trail enters from the left; stay on roadbed.

7.5 Trail forks; go left.

7.7 Trail ends at Aska Road, across from the parking lot.

Stanley Gap Trail

Location:	12 miles south of Blue Ridge, about 2 hours north of Atlanta.
Distance:	5 miles one way.
Time:	1.5 hours.
Tread:	5 miles on singletrack, some on old roadbed.
Aerobic level:	Strenuous.
Technical difficulty:	3.5.
Highlights:	Views from the highest point at 3,365 feet, sweet singletrack, excellent downhill.
Land status:	The trail lies within the Chattahoochee-Oconee National Forest, Blue Ridge District.
Maps:	USGS Blue Ridge.
Access:	From Atlanta, take Interstate 575 and Georgia Highway 515 north to Blue Ridge. From the McDonald's restaurant in Blue Ridge, continue east on GA 515 for 0.8 mile to Windy Ridge Road, where you'll turn right. Go about 0.2 mile to the dead end with old U.S. Highway 76, then turn left and go 0.2 mile to Aska Road on your right. Turn right on Aska Road and go 8 miles. Turn right onto Stanley Creek Road, across from the Toccoa River Outpost on the left. Follow the road 4.1 miles to the parking area on the right. The trail leaves from the parking area.

Notes on the trail: Previously part of the ride known as Rich Mountain, the Stanley Gap Trail is a wonderful stretch of pure Georgia mountain singletrack. The trail shares part of its length with the Benton-MacKaye Trail, one of the best hiking trails in the Southeast. After the steep, rooty initial climb, you will find yourself on a stretch of narrow singletrack cut into the steep side of the mountain. At an elevation of 3,365 feet, you're near the peak of Rocky Mountain, the high point of the ride (this is one of the higher rides in the state). The views from the ridges make the first climbs worth the effort. If you have underdressed for cold weather, you'll feel it here. The Benton-MacKaye Trail leaves the bike trail near this point.

The narrow singletrack along the higher ridges keeps your attention focused on the trail while the scenery in any season tempts you to gaze into the distance. Just past Rocky Mountain, a saddleback ridge offers a nice area for a break, with plenty of great views.

The ensuing descent is a long stretch of semitechnical singletrack that eventually joins an old forest roadbed, so that when you reach the Deep

Stanley Gap Trail

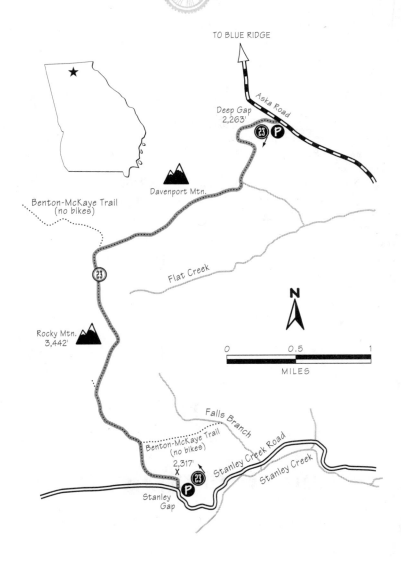

TO BLUE RIDGE

Aska Road

Deep Gap
2,263'

Davenport Mtn.

Benton-McKaye Trail
(no bikes)

Flat Creek

N

Rocky Mtn.
3,442'

0   0.5   1

MILES

Falls Branch

Benton-McKaye Trail
(no bikes)

Stanley Creek Road

2,317'
X

Stanley Creek

Stanley
Gap

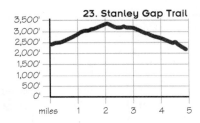

23. Stanley Gap Trail

3,500'
3,000'
2,500'
2,000'
1,500'
1,000'
500'
0'

miles   1   2   3   4   5

Gap parking area, your brakes are smoking and your hands are cramping. Definitely worth the trip.

You can use the paved Aska Road to make a loop, or carpool from Deep Gap, or do an out-and-back from either end like the "real" mountain bikers do. Any ride that includes Stanley Gap Trail is a great one!

THE RIDE

0.0 From the Stanley Gap parking area, the trail starts uphill on an old roadbed, just behind the information kiosk.

0.7 Trail joins the Benton-MacKaye Trail; go straight. Bikes are not allowed on the section that goes to the right.

2.1 High point of the ride, near the peak of Rocky Mountain.

2.8 Benton-MacKaye Trail forks to the left; bike trail continues to the right; bear right.

4.0 Stream crossing.

4.1 Trail joins an old roadbed.

4.4 Trail intersection; go left. Straight ahead is the Flat Creek Connector Trail.

4.6 Stream crossing.

4.8 Stream crossing.

4.9 Stream crossing. Just past the crossing is another intersection; turn left to go to the parking lot at Deep Gap.

5.0 Ride ends at the Deep Gap parking area.

Long Branch Loop

Location:	6 miles southeast of Blue Ridge, about 2 hours north of Atlanta.
Distance:	2.3 miles.
Time:	30 minutes.
Tread:	2.3 miles on old roadbed and doubletrack.
Aerobic level:	Easy.
Technical difficulty:	1.5.
Highlights:	Views of Green Mountain, creek crossings, excellent beginner loop.
Land status:	The trail lies within the Chattahoochee-Oconee National Forest, Toccoa District. This is a multi-use trail; please respect the rights of other users.
Maps:	USGS Blue Ridge.

Long Branch Loop

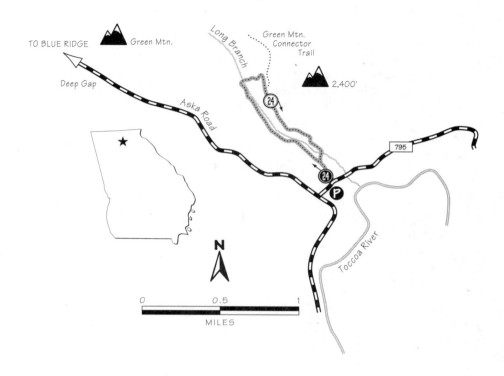

Access: From Atlanta, take Interstate 575 and Georgia Highway 515 north to Blue Ridge. From the McDonald's restaurant in Blue Ridge, continue east on GA 515 for 0.8 mile to Windy Ridge Road. Turn right and go about 0.2 mile to the dead end with old U.S. Highway 76. Turn left and go 0.2 mile to Aska Road on your right. Turn right and go south 5.9 miles to Shady Falls Road. Make a left and go 0.2 mile to the entrance to the parking lot on your left.

Notes on the trail: Just as Flat Creek isn't flat, Long Branch Loop isn't long. The trail has the distinction of being in the middle of several more difficult trails in the immediate vicinity. Because the terrain dictates so much of a trail's difficulty, it's unusual to find an easy trail so close to more difficult ones. Here's a great place to introduce someone to dirt. The trail is easy, relatively flat, and can be ridden many times or used as a warm-up for more difficult trails. If you're feeling a little stronger, ride up the Green Mountain connector trail the half mile or so to the Green Mountain Trail. It's all downhill on the way back.

The loop configuration makes it difficult to get lost, although someone probably will. The parking area is easily accessible, and the scenery in this part of the state is spectacular in the spring and fall.

If you time your ride right, you may see wild turkeys or deer along the trail. The creek crossings are easy, and the trail is almost all doubletrack or wide singletrack on roadbed, for those conversational rides. The Turkey Farm Loop is just across the road, and uses the same parking lot and starting point. You can also use this trail as an alternative access to the Green Mountain Trail. The trail's central location lends it to many ride options.

THE RIDE

0.0 The trailhead is at the end of the parking lot, next to an information kiosk.
0.1 Trail intersects with a roadbed; go left.
0.2 Roadbed forks; go left.
0.9 Views of Green Mountain.
1.3 Creek crossing.
1.4 Green Mountain Connector Trail enters from the left; stay straight on roadbed.
1.9 Roadbed forks; go right.
2.1 Creek crossing.
2.2 Roadbed enters from right rear; go left to return to parking lot.
2.3 Ride ends at parking lot.

Flat Creek Loop

Location:	About 6 miles southeast of Blue Ridge, 2 hours north of Atlanta.
Distance:	5.9 miles.
Time:	1.5 hours.
Tread:	5.9 miles on singletrack, some distances on old roadbed.
Aerobic level:	Moderate.
Technical difficulty:	3.5.
Highlights:	Lots of creek crossings, lots of rocks, some good scenery and great leaf-watching.

Land status:	The trail is located within the Chattahoochee-Oconee National Forest, Toccoa District. This is a multi-use trail; please respect the rights of other users.
Maps:	USGS Blue Ridge.
Access:	From Atlanta, take Interstate 575 and Georgia Highway 515 north to Blue Ridge. From the McDonald's restaurant in Blue Ridge, continue east on GA 515 for 0.8 mile to Windy Ridge Road. Go right on Windy Ridge Road about 0.2 mile to the dead end with Old U.S. Highway 76. Make a left and go 0.2 mile to Aska Road. Turn right onto Aska Road and go south 4.4 miles to the Deep Gap parking lot on your right, just over the crest of a hill. The trail starts from the upper end of the parking lot.

Notes on the trail: I'm not sure why they call this one Flat Creek. There's nothing flat anywhere in the immediate area, and this ride is certainly no exception.

You'll really enjoy this ride on a hot day, when the surrounding peaks shield you from the hot summer sun. Conversely, you can get pretty cold on this ride in the winter. If you always end up with wet feet on any ride like I do, take extra socks. Part of this trail follows a creek as it tumbles down along an old roadbed, and part of this trail is the creek. The numerous rocks and crossings will challenge your technical riding skill, especially if there's ice on the rocks or your rims. This loop configuration is the favorite of the locals; the ride is great in either direction.

Trying to keep the feet dry.

Flat Creek Loop

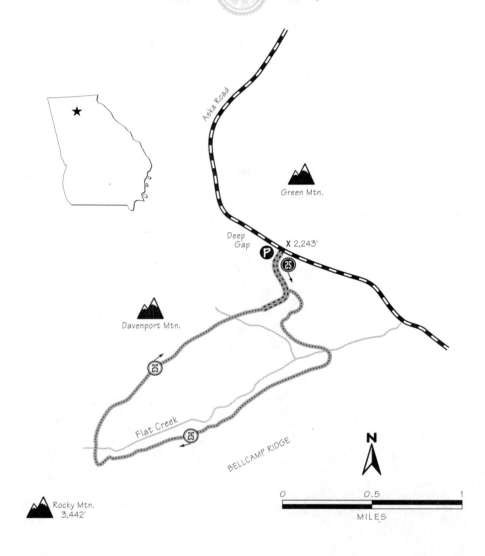

Aska Road

Green Mtn.

Deep Gap

X 2,243'

Davenport Mtn.

Flat Creek

BELLCAMP RIDGE

Rocky Mtn.
3,442'

N

0   0.5   1

MILES

25. Flat Creek Loop

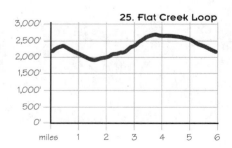

3,000'
2,500'
2,000'
1,500'
1,000'
500'
0'

miles   1   2   3   4   5   6

This trail's proximity to other great trails in the area (it shares a trailhead with the Stanley Gap Trail) makes it a great destination for all-day riding.

THE RIDE

0.0   The trailhead is on the upper end of the parking lot, next to the information sign. Follow the singletrack uphill. Just around a bend to the left, a trail enters from the right; stay on the main trail going left.

0.2   Just after a short climb on a gravel trail, go left on singletrack.

1.3   Trail joins a creek and runs parallel for a short distance.

1.6   Cross Flat Creek.

1.7   Trail joins a series of intersecting old roadbeds; follow the green and white blazes.

2.1   Series of stream crossings.

2.2   The trail begins to climb on a steep, rocky roadbed.

2.5   Two stream crossings.

2.6   Stream crossing.

2.7   Stream crossing. About 100 yards farther is a mud bog. Just after this, the trail and stream join for a short distance.

2.8   Trail forks; take the left fork (look for the green and white blazes just up the trail).

2.9   Intersection with several old roadbeds; go straight across. Look for the blazes.

3.2   Trail turns right and crosses the creek, then joins another old roadbed on the other side. Just past that is a fork; go right, still on an old roadbed.

3.5   Small mud bog. The trail becomes more of an identifiable roadbed now, and is gravel in some spots.

5.2   Stanley Gap Connector Trail enters from the left; stay right.

5.4   Trail forks to the left; go straight.

5.9   Ride ends at the parking lot.

26

Stanley Creek Loop

Location:	12 miles south of Blue Ridge, about 2 hours north of Atlanta.
Distance:	2.8 miles.
Time:	1 hour.
Tread:	1.4 miles on gravel Forest Service road and 1.4 miles on singletrack trail, some on old roadbed.
Aerobic level:	Moderately easy.
Technical difficulty:	3.5.
Highlights:	Beautiful sections along Stanley Creek, long but gradual climbs on singletrack.
Land status:	The trail is in the Chattahoochee-Oconee National Forest, Toccoa District.
Maps:	USGS Blue Ridge.
Access:	From Atlanta, take Interstate 575 and Georgia Highway 515 north to Blue Ridge. From the McDonald's restaurant in Blue Ridge, continue east on GA 515 for 0.8 mile to Windy Ridge Road. Go right on Windy Ridge about 0.2 mile to the dead end with Old U.S. Highway 76. Turn left and go 0.2 mile to Aska Road on your right. Make a right onto Aska Road and travel 8 miles. Turn right onto Stanley Creek Road, across from the Toccoa River Outpost on the left. Follow Stanley Creek Road 4.1 miles to the parking area on the right.

Notes on the trail: Stanley Creek Trail is a good example of a short but tough North Georgia trail. The singletrack section runs on old logging road-beds that seem to be all over the place in these parts, although the trail is so overgrown in some sections, you wouldn't believe too many folks had been there before.

The section that loosely follows Stanley Creek is a beautiful trail, and some sections have some rocky surprises for you if you don't pay attention. The gravel return leg on Forest Road 330 opens up some views of the surrounding peaks, and gives you a good sampling of the local terrain.

The section that runs along Stanley Creek is full of photo opportunities in the fall. Don't forget your camera.

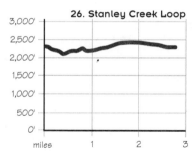

Stanley Creek Loop

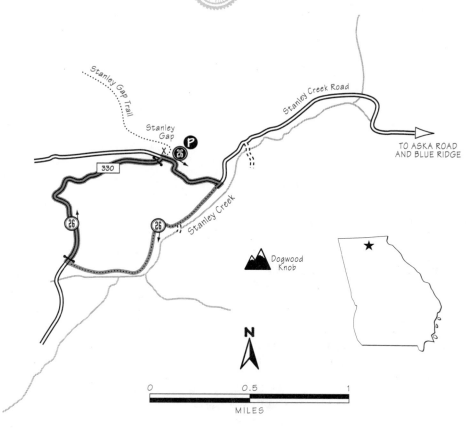

THE RIDE

0.0 From the parking lot at Stanley Gap, ride back along the gravel road, down the hill. The grade is steep here, but you'll turn off soon, so pay attention!

0.4 A roadbed enters from the right rear; turn sharp right and follow the roadbed.

0.5 Stream crossing. Just across the stream, the trail forks right, off the roadbed.

0.8 Several roadbeds fork; take the middle left fork up the hill. Trail turns left and leaves the roadbed; follow it left, onto a downhill technical section.

0.9 Stream crossing; technical section ends at the creek; bear right on the roadbed.

1.1 Roadbed forks right; stay left on the trail.

1.15 Trail forks left off another roadbed; go left.

1.3 Stream crossing.

1.6 Stream crossing. Just past the stream a roadbed enters from the right; go straight.

1.7 Trail ends at a gated forest road. Turn right, around the gate and along the road.

2.6 Forest road intersects another gravel road at a gate; turn right onto the gravel road.

2.8 Turn left into Stanley Gap parking lot.

Turkey Farm Loop

Location:	6 miles southeast of Blue Ridge, 2 hours north of Atlanta.
Distance:	4.7 miles.
Time:	1 hour.
Tread:	0.8 mile on paved road, 0.9 mile trail on old roadbed, and 3 miles on gravel Forest Service roads.
Aerobic level:	Moderately easy.
Technical difficulty:	1.5.
Highlights:	Old farmstead, winding forest roads, lake views.
Land status:	The roads border or lie within the Chattahoochee-Oconee National Forest, Blue Ridge District. This is a multi-use trail; please respect the rights of other users.
Maps:	USGS Blue Ridge.
Access:	From Atlanta, take Interstate 575 and Georgia Highway 515 north to Blue Ridge. From the McDonald's restaurant in Blue Ridge, continue east on GA 515 for 0.8 mile to Windy Ridge Road. Turn right onto Windy Ridge Road and go about 0.2 mile to the dead end with old U.S. Highway 76. Turn left and travel 0.2 mile to Aska Road on your right. Make a right and go south 5.9 miles to Shady Falls Road: turn left and go 0.2 mile to the entrance to the parking lot on your left.

Notes on the trail: The Turkey Farm ride uses gravel forest roads, a gated section of forest road, a winding trail on roadbed through an old farmstead, and a short section of paved road to make an excellent beginner ride and all-weather loop.

The forest road follows the shoreline of Blue Ridge Lake for some distance, and you can see some beautiful private homes along the way. The forest road on the other side the loop reveals great views of the higher peaks in the area, and reminds you of more strenuous rides for other days. The

Turkey Farm Loop

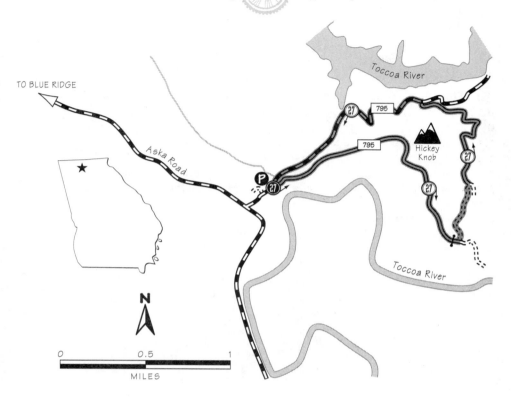

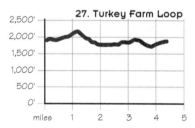

leaf-watching on this ride is spectacular in high season. The first downhill section to the gate has some deceptively tricky, dozer-built, launching pad-grade dips. The section running through the old farmstead is one of the most pleasant miles of riding in the area. The foundations of old farm buildings give cause for reflection on past uses of the land while you roll through. Three highly vigilant and dedicated dogs make the first section of gravel forest road pass much more quickly. Just as you catch your breath, you encounter the first of the two climbs on the ride.

All in all, this is an entertaining alternative to muddy trails on a wet winter's day, and a great beginner loop any time of year. The listed forest and county roads are open to motorized traffic.

THE RIDE

0.0 From the parking lot, continue along the paved Shady Falls Road for 0.1 mile.

0.1 Turn right on Turkey Farm Road, Forest Road 795.

0.4 Road to the right; stay straight on FR 795.

1.1 View of Stanley Gap and Deep Gap to your right.

1.5 Road to the left; stay straight on FR 795.

1.7 Gate at a turnaround; go around the gate and continue along the roadbed.

1.8 Road enters a clearing and continues straight; turn left here and follow another roadbed.

2.4 Stream crossing.

2.6 Trail intersects with a gravel road; turn left.

3.0 Intersection with another gravel road; turn left.

3.7 Intersection with a paved road; turn left.

3.8 Pavement ends; continue on gravel road.

4.0 Gravel road ends at Shady Falls Road; turn left and ride uphill.

4.7 Ride ends back at the parking lot.

Dahlonega

The Bull Mountain area, near Dahlonega, offers some of the most popular riding areas in northern Georgia. Located in the Toccoa District of the Chattahoochee-Oconee National Forest, the area's trails are located primarily in recreation areas, although some of the trails either run next to or across wildlife management areas. The riding opportunities range from well-maintained forest roads that can be ridden year-round, to tight, twisty, technical singletrack that is best left to drier conditions.

The Bull Mountain, Bare Hare, Turner Creek, No-Tell, and Jones Creek Ridge trails are the result of cooperation between the USDA Forest Service, SORBA, and the Chattahoochee Trail Riders Association (CTRA), an equestrian group. Both user groups are the primary source for maintenance of the existing trails, and both are participating in the construction of almost 30 miles of new trails. The excellent trail opportunities in this area will continue to be exploited over the next several years.

Bull Mountain enjoys a well-deserved reputation for some of the best riding in the state. Also check out nearby Dahlonega, which has a rich and interesting history as one of the original gold rush towns, and offers many restaurants and lodging options. If you or your significant other likes browsing through craft shops, Christmas shops, and other such diversions, Dahlonega will keep you occupied for a while. Just get your riding in first, or you may not get it in at all.

Cruising on Bull Mountain.

Bull Mountain Loop

Location:	7 miles west of Dahlonega, about 1 hour from Atlanta
Distance:	14.5 miles.
Time:	2.5 hours.
Tread:	2.8 miles on singletrack, 2.6 miles on gravel road, 2 miles on jeep road, and 7.1 miles on singletrack on old roadbed.
Aerobic level:	Moderate.
Technical difficulty:	3. A couple of tricky creek crossings, zillions of rocks, and a twisting, rooty, off-camber, singletrack downhill.
Highlights:	A classic northern Georgia trail with lots of climbs and downhills, and plenty of options.
Land status:	The entire area is located within the Chattahoochee-Oconee National Forest, Blue Ridge District. This is a multi-use trail; please respect the rights of other users.
Maps:	USGS Nimblewill and Campbell Mountain.
Access:	From Atlanta, follow U.S. Highway 19/Georgia Highway 400 north about 46 miles to GA 136. Turn left and drive 6.5 miles to GA 9, then go right and drive 4.7 miles north (toward Dahlonega) to GA 52. Turn left (toward Ellijay) on GA 52 and drive 7.5 miles to Grizzle's Store (abandoned) on the right. At the store turn right; there will be a sign for Nimblewill Baptist Church on the right. Follow the paved road 3.2 miles to Forest Road 28 (gravel) on your right. Turn right onto FR 28 and go about 0.2 mile. Take the first dirt road left—FR 83—and drive 1.5 miles to the gravel parking lot on the right. Park here and pedal to the trailhead, about 0.3 mile north on FR 83 on your left.

Notes on the trail: Bull Mountain Trail consists of alternating single- and doubletrack, with long steady climbs and shorter, steeper downhills. The original trail used Lance Creek Road, a gated Forest Service road, to complete a loop. The recently completed Bare Hare Trail replaces Lance Creek Road as the return route (although you can still use Lance Creek Road as an easy midride bailout) with a long, steady, rocky doubletrack climb, followed by a long, twisty, undulating singletrack downhill, followed by a fast, twisting,

Bull Mountain Loop

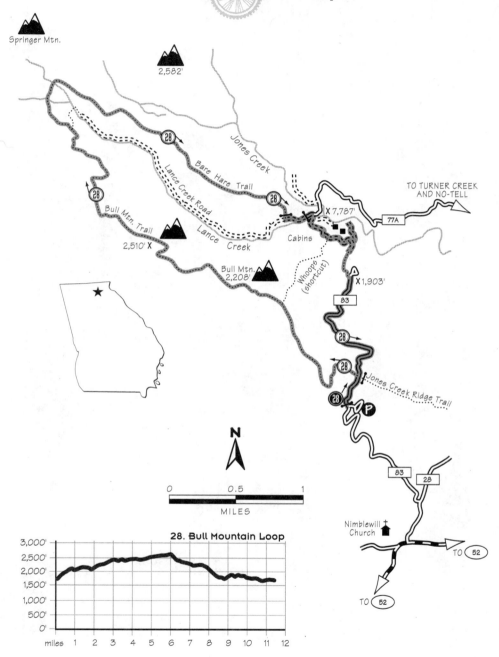

Springer Mtn.

2,582'

Jones Creek

28

Bare Hare Trail

Lance Creek Road

28

TO TURNER CREEK
AND NO-TELL

77A

X 7,787'

Cabins

Bull Mtn. Trail

2,510' X

Lance Creek

Bull Mtn.
2,208'

Whoops
(shortcut)

X 1,903'

83

28

28

Jones Creek Ridge Trail

28

P

83   28

Nimblewill
Church

TO 52

TO 52

N

| 0 | 0.5 | 1 |

MILES

28. Bull Mountain Loop

3,000'
2,500'
2,000'
1,500'
1,000'
500'
0'

miles 1 2 3 4 5 6 7 8 9 10 11 12

Peace and love on the Bull Mountain Loop.

eye-watering fire road descent back to Lance Creek. There is one larger creek crossing and several smaller ones through the course of this ride.

During late spring, mountain laurel blooms along the upper reaches of Bare Hare's climb and descent. Just north of the northern-most section of Bare Hare Trail lies Springer Mountain, the southern terminus of the Appalachian Trail. There are several scenic viewpoints along the lower reaches of Lance Creek. If you're quiet, you can hear one of the many hidden waterfalls along the upper sections of Lance Creek. It is not unusual to surprise deer or wild turkeys along the quieter sections of trail. It's not hard to see why this is one of the most popular rides in northern Georgia.

THE RIDE

0.0 From the parking lot, pedal north 0.3 mile on FR 83. The trailhead will be on your left.

0.3 Turn left onto Bull Mountain Trail.

1.4 Trail forks; take the left fork up the mountain. (The right fork connects with the trail intersection mentioned at mile 10.9 below, allowing a much shorter option.)

2.5 Trail enters from the left; continue straight.

3.9 Wildlife opening on the right.

5.9 Trail forks. Take the left fork to continue on Bare Hare Trail. To the right, down a steep section and through a gate is Lance Creek Road. Use this option for an early bailout.

6.4 Creek crossing.

6.7 Creek crossing.

6.8 Creek crossing.

7.0 Steep hike-a-bike section. Singletrack downhill begins at the top.

8.6 Trail opens into a large wildlife opening. The doubletrack continues on the far left side of the clearing.

10.1 Forest service gate at Lance Creek Road. Go left.

10.3 Forest service gate. Turn right and ford Lance Creek, then take the right doubletrack fork.

10.4 Roadbed forks; go left.

10.9 Roadbed forks to the right. Stay left on the doubletrack (see mile 1.4).

11.2 Hunting cabin on the left (private property). Doubletrack continues straight, and a roadbed forks to the right. Take this right fork.

11.7 Hunting cabin on the left.

12.3 Doubletrack ends at "No Bikes/Horses" sign. Look for a short section of singletrack on your right. Turn right here.

12.4 Turn right on FR 83.

14.2 Trailhead on the right.

14.5 Ride ends at the parking lot.

Jones Creek Ridge Trail

Location:	About 7 miles west of Dahlonega, about 1.5 hours from Atlanta.
Distance:	3.3 miles.
Time:	45 minutes.
Tread:	1.3 miles on gravel forest road, 1.1 miles on singletrack, and 0.9 mile on singletrack on old logging roadbeds.
Aerobic level:	Moderate.
Technical difficulty:	2.5.
Highlights:	Singletrack trail along a ridge, a beautiful mountain lake, lots of mountain laurel.
Land status:	The trail is located within the Chattahoochee-Oconee National Forest, Toccoa District. This is a multi-use trail; please respect the rights of other users.
Maps:	USGS Nimblewill.
Access:	From Atlanta, drive north on U.S. Highway 19/Georgia Highway 400 about 46 miles to GA 136. Turn left and drive 6.5 miles to GA 9, then go right and drive 4.7 miles north on GA 9 (toward Dahlonega) to GA 52. Turn left (toward Ellijay) and drive 7.5 miles west on GA 52 to Grizzle's Store (abandoned) on the right. Turn right at the store; there will be a sign for Nimblewill Baptist Church on the right. Follow the paved road 3.2 miles to Forest Road 28 (gravel) on your right. Turn right on FR 28 and take the first dirt road left—FR 83—and drive 1.5 miles to the gravel parking lot on the right. Park here and pedal 0.3 mile to the trailhead on FR 83 on your right.

Notes on the trail: Jones Creek Ridge Trail was completed in 1998 through the cooperation of SORBA and the Chattahoochee Trail Horse Association, in order to connect the Bull Mountain trails with Turner Creek and No-Tell trails, and with planned trail additions along the southeastern side of FR 28. While created primarily to get horse and bike traffic off of the busy Forest Service roads, the trail itself is a pleasure to ride. The trail crosses a dam by a man-made lake with views of the surrounding mountains reflecting off the water on a calm day. The upper section is awash in mountain laurel. The trail alternates off and on an old roadbed, creating a varied and interesting ride. You'll skirt a large wildlife opening with ample opportunity to view some of the local creatures in their home habitat. While mapping this

Jones Creek Ridge Trail •
No-Tell Loop •
Turner Creek Loop

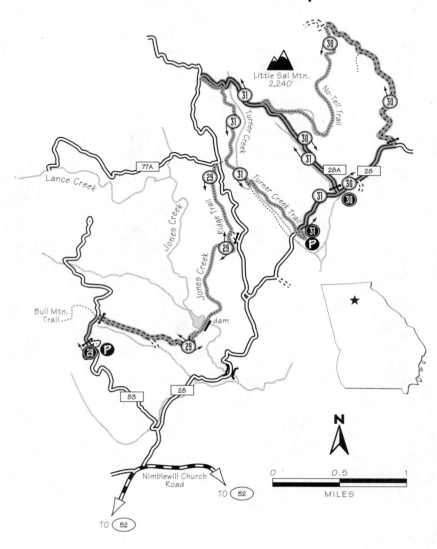

Little Sal Mtn.
2,240'

No-Tell Trail

Turner Creek

Turner Creek Trail

Lance Creek

Jones Creek

Ridge Trail

Jones Creek

Bull Mtn.
Trail

dam

N

0   0.5   1

MILES

Nimblewill Church
Road

TO 52

TO 52

Jones Creek Ridge Trail.

trail, I was buzzed by four wild turkeys with attitudes one winter's day. Guess I interrupted something important.

THE RIDE

0.0 From the parking lot, pedal 0.3 mile north on FR 83. A gated roadbed will be on your right, directly across from the Bull Mountain Trailhead. Go right, around the gate.

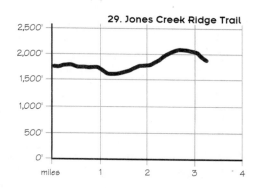

29. Jones Creek Ridge Trail

0.4 Roadbed forks right; stay left.

0.9 Roadbed skirts a wildlife opening to the right.

1.2 Follow the trail across the dam.

1.3 Roadbed enters a large wildlife opening; look for the trail skirting the right side of the field.

1.6 Trail enters the woods to the right at the top of the field.

2.4 Singletrack ends at a roadbed; turn left and follow the roadbed up the hill.

2.6 Trail skirts another wildlife opening and rejoins the roadbed on the other side.

3.1 Trail forks; go left.

3.2 Roadbed enters from the right; stay left.

3.3 Trail ends at the intersection of FR 77 and FR 77A. From here you can connect to Turner Creek Trail, or retrace your tracks to return to the trailhead.

No-Tell Loop

See Map
on Page 103

Location: 7 miles west of Dahlonega, about 1 hour from Atlanta.

Distance: 2.9 miles.

Time: 30 minutes.

Tread: 1.5 miles on gravel Forest Service road, 0.6 mile on singletrack, and 0.8 mile on logging roadbed.

Aerobic level: Moderately easy.

Technical difficulty: 2. (Excess speed can make this a 4.)

Highlights: All climbing is at the start of the ride; downhill singletrack twisties to finish.

Land status:	The trail is in the Chattahoochee-Oconee National Forest, Toccoa District. This is a multi-use trail; please respect the rights of other users.
Maps:	USGS Campbell Mountain.
Access:	From Atlanta, drive north on U.S. Highway 19/Georgia Highway 400 about 46 miles to GA 136. Turn left on GA 136 and drive 6.5 miles to GA 9. Turn right and drive 4.7 miles north (toward Dahlonega) to GA 52. Turn left (toward Ellijay) on GA 52 and drive 7.5 miles to Grizzle's Store (abandoned) on right. Turn right at the store; there will be a sign for Nimblewill Baptist Church on the right. Follow the paved road 3.2 miles to Forest Road 28 (gravel) on your right. Turn right and follow FR 28 for 2.3 miles to the second gated road to the left, FR 28A. Park along the road.

Notes on the trail: No-Tell Trail starts with a moderate climb along the main forest road, then climbs farther along a gated jeep road to the highest point. The singletrack starts here, launching you into a roller-coaster downhill, which deposits you breathless and charged on another gated forest road. It's an easy spin past wildlife openings and along a creek back to the start. A great beginner loop!

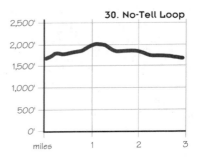

THE RIDE

0.0   Pedal northeast along FR 28 for 0.5 mile. Just over a hill, you'll find another gated jeep road to the left. Go left around the gate and follow the roadbed.

0.7   Wildlife opening to the left.

1.0   Roadbed enters from the left, stay straight on the main roadbed.

1.3   Singletrack leaves trail to the left, going downhill; go left and hang on!

1.9   Singletrack ends at FR 28A; go left. (Go right if you want to connect with Turner Creek Trail and make a longer loop.)

2.1   Wildlife opening to the right.

2.7   Wildlife opening to the left.

2.9   Ride ends at the gate at FR 28.

Turner Creek Loop

See Map
on Page 103

Location: 7 miles west of Dahlonega, about 1 hour from Atlanta.

Distance: 4.4 miles.

Time: 1 hour

Tread: 2.3 miles on gravel forest roads, and 2.1 miles on singletrack, some on old logging roadbed.

Aerobic level: Moderate.

Technical difficulty: 3.

Land status: The trail is located within the Chattahoochee-Oconee National Forest, Toccoa District. This is a multi-use trail; please respect the rights of other users.

Maps: USGS Nimblewill and Campbell Mountain.

Access: From Atlanta, drive north on U.S. Highway 19/ Georgia Highway 400 about 46 miles to GA 136. Turn left and drive 6.5 miles west to GA 9, where you'll turn right (toward Dahlonega) and drive 4.7 miles to GA 52. Turn left (toward Ellijay) on GA 52 and drive 7.5 miles west to Grizzle's Store (abandoned) on the right. Turn right at the store; there will be a sign for Nimblewill Baptist Church on the right. Follow the paved road 3.2 miles to Forest Road 28 (gravel) on your right. Turn right onto FR 28 and drive 2.1 miles until you cross the third creek. Park just beyond the bridge on the right.

Notes on the trail: Turner Creek Trail is a mostly downhill singletrack connector trail between Forest Service roads. This loop trail is one of SORBA's favorite beginner rides.

The loop is like a roller coaster—after the initial forest road climb to the top, it's a fun ride down, and a sensory feast for the second half. The singletrack section of the trail is narrow, fast, and tight, and travels through several mini-ecosystems along its short length. Part of the trail runs through a fern-filled glade; another follows rushing Turner Creek along the lower section, with two small bridge crossings. I've seen more wild turkeys on this trail than on any other.

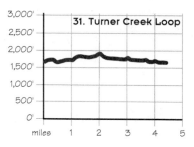

Turner Creek Loop.

THE RIDE

0.0 Pedal northeast along FR 28.

0.5 Turn left at the first gated forest road to your left (FR 28A) and follow the gravel forest road up the hill.

0.7 Wildlife opening to the right.

1.5 No-Tell Trail enters from the right (see Ride 30). Stay on FR 28A.

2.1 Wildlife opening to the right.

2.2 Road forks to the right; stay left.

2.3 Trailhead on your left. Go left on singletrack.

2.7 Footbridge.

3.2 Bridge or remains of bridge.

3.3 Trail forks right; stay left.

3.4 Trail joins an old logging roadbed.

3.8 Trail enters from the left. Bikes turn left (horses must stay on the logging roadbed).

3.9 Bridge.

4.4 Trail ends at FR 28.

Montgomery Creek Loop

Location:	7 miles west of Dahlonega, about 1.5 hours north of Atlanta.
Distance:	8.5 miles.
Time:	1.5 hours.
Tread:	8.5 miles on gravel Forest Service roads.
Aerobic level:	Moderately easy.
Technical difficulty:	1.5.
Highlights:	Two creek crossings, a beautiful forest, and peace and quiet.
Land status:	The trail is located within the Chattahoochee-Oconee National Forest, Blue Ridge District. This is a multi-use trail; please respect the rights of other users.
Maps:	USGS Nimblewill and Campbell Mountain.
Access:	From Atlanta, drive north on U.S. Highway 19/Georgia Highway 400 about 46 miles to GA 136. Turn left and drive 6.5 miles to GA 9, then turn right (toward Dahlonega) and drive 4.7 miles to GA 52. Make a left and drive 7.5 miles west on GA 52 to Grizzle's Store (abandoned) on the right. Turn right on Nimblewill Church Road and follow it for 3.2 miles to Forest Road 28 (gravel) on your right. Turn right and drive 2.4 miles on FR 28 to the fourth gated road to your left. Park off the road at this intersection.

Notes on the trail: Consisting entirely of gravel Forest Service roads, this ride is great for beginners, or anyone who has made the drive to the area only to find rain or hopelessly muddy trails. The road winds gently through a varying forest, with a few short climbs to remind you that you're on a bike, and a few descents to remind you of the rewards.

The two creek crossings are easy, and there's a nice picnic spot at the first creek crossing. The section of FR 28 along the Etowah River is a reward in itself, if you like mountain creeks like I do. This ride is one of the best for carrying on a conversation with your riding partners.

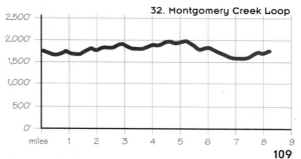

Montgomery Creek Loop

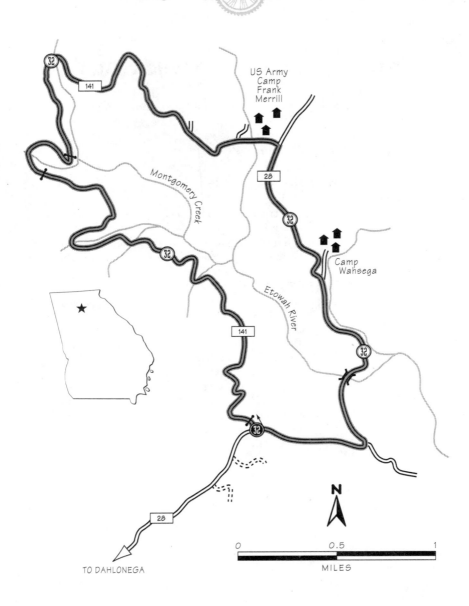

US Army
Camp
Frank
Merrill

Montgomery Creek

141

28

32

32

Camp
Wahsega

Etowah River

141

32

32

★

32

28

TO DAHLONEGA

N

0   0.5   1
MILES

0.0 Go around the gate and onto FR 141.

0.8 Wildlife opening to the right.

1.2 Road passes through a wildlife opening.

1.3 Enter another wildlife opening.

2.2 Pass through a gate.

2.7 Enter another wildlife opening.

3.3 Creek crossing.

5.3 Road enters from the left; stay on the main gravel road.

5.6 Road enters from the right; stay on the main gravel road.

5.7 Gated road to the left; stay on the main gravel road. You are now on part of the Army Ranger camp.

5.8 Creek crossing.

5.9 Intersection with FR 28; go right on FR 28.

6.6 Pass Camp Wahsega on your left. The road runs along the creek for a short distance.

7.4 Road enters from the right; stay on FR 28 and cross the bridge over the Etowah River.

7.5 Intersection with FR 72 to the left; stay right on FR 28.

8.5 Ride ends back at FR 141.

Helen

Northeast of Dahlonega is the town of Helen. If you liked the shops and such in Dahlonega, you'll love Helen. The town is built to resemble a Bavarian village, with the buildings along the main street and downtown area exhibiting a quaint and semi-realistic facade that takes on an even more colorful look at night and during festivals.

The restaurants and lodging are plentiful here, and Helen offers its own annual version of Oktoberfest every fall, complete with polkas and nightly celebrations.

Lest you write the town off as just a sedentary shopper-type tourist destination, remember that Helen has hosted several National Off-Road Bicycle Association national series races, and a World Cup race on the course at Unicoi State Park. The Upper Chattahoochee, Jasus Creek, and Hickory Nut trails are all great rides as well, and the scenery is fantastic, especially during fall.

The town offers lots of options for that after-ride snarfing of any food item in sight, and boasts an excellent fudge shop. (You have to hunt for it.)

The town has its own bike shop and tour operator, Woody's, and its own SORBA chapter, which does a great deal of the maintenance on the area trails. Stop in and see Woody for some inside local info, to volunteer to help out with the trails, or to find the fudge shop.

Helen, like Dahlonega, is one of those destinations my wife loves to accompany me to, as long as I don't actually expect her to ride.

Unicoi State Park Bike Trail

Location:	In Helen, about 2 hours north of Atlanta.
Distance:	7.4 miles.
Time:	1.5 hours
Tread:	7.4 miles on wide singletrack on old roadbed.
Aerobic level:	Moderately strenuous.
Technical difficulty:	3.
Highlights:	A NORBA race course, great trail, excellent fudge shop in town.
Land status:	The trail is located in Unicoi State Park.

Maps: USGS Helen.

Access: From Atlanta, go north on Georgia Highway 400 to the end of the four-lane. Continue straight 4.6 miles on Long Branch Road, then turn right onto GA 52 and drive 2 miles to a fork in the road. Go left on GA 115 and drive 10.5 miles to downtown Cleveland. Turn left around the square in Cleveland and follow signs to GA 75, about 0.3 mile from the square. Go right on GA 75 and drive the 8 miles to Helen. Continue through Helen on GA 75 and in about 1.1 miles look for the sign for Unicoi State Park, a right turn on GA 356. Follow GA 356 into the park, and stop at the lodge office for your rider number. From the office, continue along GA 356 to the first paved road right after the lodge. Turn right to the tennis court parking area. Park here; the trailhead is just down the drive to the maintenance shed, at a small creek crossing.

Notes on the trail: If you've ever wondered what it's like to race on a NORBA-level race course, here's your chance. The trail was built for racing, and it shows. This is a ride that keeps your attention throughout because of the constant elevation changes and difficult sections of trail. You can get a good idea of what professional racers face by riding this trail, and you'll gain a great deal of respect for their talents after a lap or two. Imagine the water crossings without the bridges, and you'll have even more respect.

The trail is not all business, though. There are several scenic sections along the creeks, and some view possibilities at the high points. The entire trail is a pleasure to ride, because of its apparent isolation while being so close to civilization. For even greater scenery, come here in the fall, when the colors are at their peak, but the ride is well worth the trip any time of year. There is a $2 fee to ride the trail, payable at the lodge office.

THE RIDE

0.0 From the parking area, go down the gravel drive by the maintenance shed. You'll see the trailhead just past the roadbed.

0.2 Cross a bridge over the creek. Just across the bridge, the trail crosses a gravel road.

1.3 Trail forks; go right.

1.7 Trail intersects another trail from the left; go right. The trail enters a powerline cut on an old roadbed.

2.1 Trail leaves the powerline cut and roadbed and turns uphill to the left.

2.3 Trail runs along a creek.

2.5 Cross a bridge over the creek. At the fork across the bridge, go right.

3.0 Trail enters from the left; go right.

3.9 Trail crosses an old roadbed.

Unicoi State Park Bike Trail

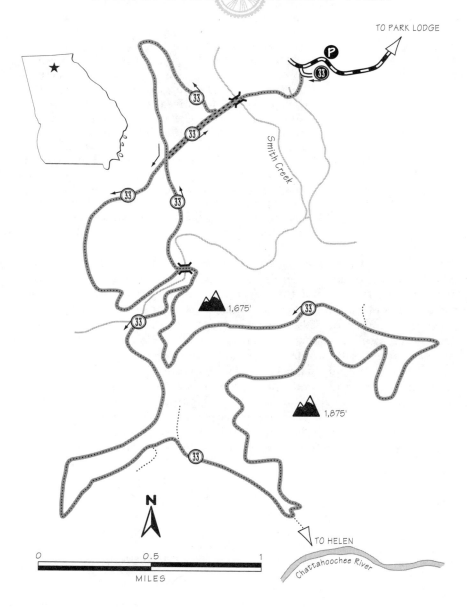

TO PARK LODGE

Smith Creek

1,675'

1,875'

N

TO HELEN

Chattahoochee River

0   0.5   1

MILES

33. Unicoi State Park Bike Trail

2,500'
2,000'
1,500'
1,000'
500'
0'

miles 1 2 3 4 5 6 7 8

4.1	Intersection with a hiking trail; go straight across.
4.3	Cross a bridge over a creek.
4.5	Trail forks; to the right is the connector trail to Helen. Go left for the loop.
5.6	Trail intersection; go left up the hill.
5.7	Hiking trail forks to the right; stay left on the roadbed.
6.1	Trail intersection; go straight.
6.2	Trail forks and switches back to the right; go right.
6.5	Cross a bridge over the creek. After you cross the bridge, turn right.
6.8	Trail joins an old roadbed; pass old cabin ruins.
7.0	Trail intersects from the left; go straight.
7.1	Cross gravel road, then cross a bridge over the creek.
7.4	Ride ends at the trailhead.

Upper Chattahoochee Loop

Location: About 4 miles northwest of Helen, 2 hours from Atlanta.

Distance: 15.6 miles.

Time: 3 hours.

Tread: 15.6 miles on gravel forest road; some gated.

Aerobic level: Moderate.

Technical difficulty: 2.

Highlights: Upper reaches of the Chattahoochee River, overlooks, long downhills.

Land status: The loop is in the Chattahoochee-Oconee National Forest, Chattooga District.

Maps: USGS Cowrock and Jack's Gap.

Access: From Atlanta, go north on Georgia Highway 400 to the end of the four lane. Continue straight 4.6 miles on Long Branch Road, then turn right onto GA 52 and drive 2 miles to a fork in the road. Go left on GA 115 and drive 10.5 miles to downtown Cleveland. Turn left around the square in Cleveland and follow signs to GA 75, about 0.3 mile from the square. Go right on GA 75 and drive the 8 miles to Helen. From Helen, go about 1 mile north on GA 75 to the intersection of GA Alt75 and Forest Road 44. Turn left, cross the river, and turn right on FR 44. Follow FR 44 for 2.9 miles to the game check station. The ride starts here.

Upper Chattahoochee Loop

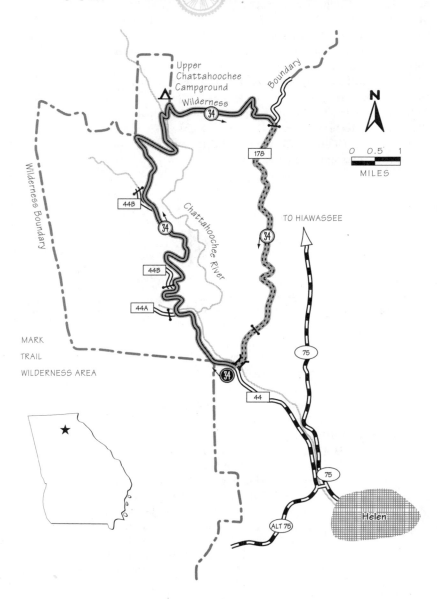

Notes on the trail: If you like forest road loops, overlooks, mountain creeks and waterfalls, and long downhills, you're going to love this ride. Starting from the game check station, you'll climb somewhat gradually on an open gravel forest road that roughly parallels the upper reaches of the Chattahoochee River. The scenery is almost enough to help you forget you're climbing, and there are plenty of good rest stops along the way.

You'll pass the Upper Chattahoochee Campground, an excellent spot for camping, then climb some more until you intersect with a gated forest road. This is the start of the real fun; this road is little used and not open to motorized traffic most of the time. The surface is less gravel and more dirt, and some sections get a little steep and twisty. Let 'er rip and enjoy the ensuing series of downhills. You've earned them! The ride ends with a short climb back to the game check station.

Restrictions: The listed forest roads are open to motorized traffic. Some sections of this loop are located within a wildlife management area and the trails are closed during scheduled hunt days. Please check the bulletin boards at the game check station, or call the number listed in Appendix C for information.

THE RIDE

0.0 From the game check station, continue uphill along FR 44.
1.3 FR 44A continues straight. Instead, turn right and cross a bridge over Low Gap Creek.
1.6 FR 44B enters from the left; continue on FR 44.
2.5 FR 44 turns right and crosses a bridge.
3.7 FR 44B enters from the left; stay on FR 44.
4.7 Road to right into undeveloped camping area; stay on FR 44.
4.8 Wildlife opening to the right.
5.2 Another wildlife opening to the right.
5.4 FR 44C enters from the left; stay on FR 44.

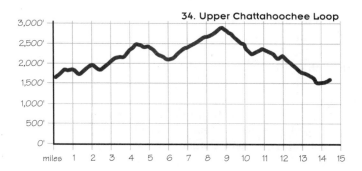

Chatahoochee River National Recreation Area.

5.9 Waterfall to the right.

6.5 Cross a bridge over the river.

6.7 Upper Chattahoochee Campground to the left. Continue on FR 44.

7.5 Waterfall to the right.

8.6 Cross a bridge over the creek.

9.5 Gated FR 178 enters from the right; turn right

9.8 Wildlife opening and overlook to the right.

10.1 Overlook to the left.

10.4 Wildlife opening to the left.

10.5 Clearcut to right; view of the mountain you just rode up.

10.6 Roadbed forks right; stay left.

10.8 Whoop-dee-doos and rougher road section. Enjoy!

10.9 Roadbed to the left to a wildlife opening; stay right.

11.4 Roadbed to the left; go straight.

11.8 Wildlife opening to the left.

12.2 Overlook to the right.

12.8 Pass through a gate.

12.9 Roadbed goes left; stay right.

13.2 Roadbed to the left; go straight.

13.8 Gated Forest Service road enters from the left rear; stay straight.

14.8 Cross a bridge across the river and turn right on FR 44.

15.6 Ride ends at the game check station.

Jasus Creek Loop

Location:	About 4 miles northwest of Helen, 2 hours from Atlanta.
Distance:	12 miles.
Time:	2 hours.
Tread:	12 miles on gravel forest road, some gated.
Aerobic level:	Moderately easy.
Technical difficulty:	1.5.
Highlights:	First section follows the upper reaches of the Chattahoochee River, lots of wildlife potential.
Land status:	The trail is in the Chattahoochee-Oconee National Forest, Chatooga District.
Maps:	USGS Cowrock and Jack's Gap.
Access:	From Atlanta, go north on Georgia Highway 400 to the end of the four lane. Continue straight 4.6 miles on Long Branch Road, then turn right onto GA 52 and drive 2 miles to a fork in the road. Go left on GA 115 and drive 10.5 miles to downtown Cleveland. Turn left around the square in Cleveland and follow signs to GA 75, about 0.3 mile from the square. Go right on GA 75 and drive the 8 miles to Helen. From Helen, go north on GA 75 about 1 mile to the intersection of GA Alt75 and Forest Road 44. Turn left, cross the river, and turn right on FR 44. Follow FR 44 for 2.9 miles to the game check station. The ride starts here.

Notes on the trail: The first thing that will get your attention on this ride is the scenery along the Chattahoochee River as the road follows it for some distance. It's one of North Georgia's more scenic stretches of forest road, and the sound of rushing water will serenade you as you climb along the first section of the ride.

Relax! The ride is an up-and-down, almost all

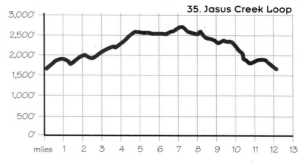

35. Jasus Creek Loop

Jasus Creek Loop

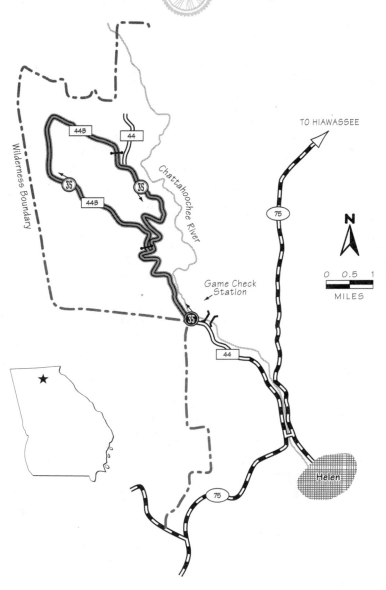

downhill for the second half. There are some sections of very large gravel that will definitely get your attention on the way back down, but other than that, just enjoy the surroundings.

This is an excellent strong beginner's ride for poor weather, or just rolling along and enjoying a social ride and enjoying the scenery. Bring a camera.

Restrictions: The listed forest roads are open to motorized traffic. Some sections of this loop are located within a wildlife management area, the trails are closed during scheduled hunt days. Please check the bulletin boards at the game check station, or call the number listed in Appendix C for information

---

THE RIDE

0.0 From the game check station, continue uphill along FR 44.

1.3 FR 44A goes straight. Instead, turn right and cross a bridge over Low Gap Creek.

1.6 FR 44B enters from the left; continue on FR 44.

2.5 FR 44 turns right and crosses a bridge.

3.7 FR 44B enters from the left; turn left and go up FR 44B.

4.7 Top of the worst climb; it's fun from here.

5.4 Wildlife opening to the left.

6.2 Road crosses a creek over a culvert.

6.9 Roadbed enters from the right; stay straight on FR 44B.

7.2 Roadbed enters from the left; stay straight on FR 44B

7.5 Roadbed enters from the right; stay straight on FR 44B.

8.1 Large teeth-rattling gravel section.

9.4 Wildlife opening to the left.

9.8 Large teeth-rattling gravel section.

10.4 Intersection with FR 44; turn right on FR 44.

10.7 Cross the bridge and go left on FR 44 (FR 44A goes right).

12.0 Ride ends at the game check station.

Hickory Nut Trail Loop

Location:	Just outside of Helen, 2 hours north of Atlanta.
Distance:	18 miles.
Time:	3 hours.
Tread:	10.4 miles on gravel forest road, 4.5 miles on gated former forest road, and 3.1 miles of paved road.
Aerobic level:	Strenuous.
Technical difficulty:	4.
Highlights:	Long initial climb, great overlooks, lots of waterfalls and creeks, killer downhill.
Land status:	The trail lies within the Chattahoochee-Oconee National Forest, Chattooga District.
Maps:	USGS Tray Mountain and Helen.
Access:	From Atlanta, go north on Georgia Highway 400 to the end of the four lane. Continue straight 4.6 miles on Long Branch Road, then turn right onto GA 52 and drive 2 miles to a fork in the road. Go left on GA 115 and drive 10.5 miles to downtown Cleveland. Turn left around the square in Cleveland and follow signs to GA 75, about 0.3 mile from the square. Go right on GA 75 and drive the 8 miles to Helen. From the bridge over the river in downtown Helen, go west along GA 75 for 1.1 miles, then turn right on GA 356. Go 0.1 mile and turn left. Look for Woody's Bike Shop on the left. The ride starts at the bike shop.

Notes on the trail: Okay, hammerheads, you want to train? You want pain? Tired of these wussy 12-milers? Then here's your ride! Hickory Nut Trail and Loop is the creation of the members of the Helen-SORBA chapter, who obviously are in pretty decent shape.

The first 8.5 miles climb steadily up a gravel forest road, finally nearing the top of Tray Mountain at around 3,800 feet elevation, (the ride starts at 1,570 feet). At the top of the mountain, the reward starts. The next 7 miles are literally all downhill. The gravel forest road at the top of the mountain turns off onto an old roadbed filled with steep torrents of babyhead rocks and technical challenges, and it deteriorates from there. If you're distracted by the climb or the scenery, you'll pay for it along these sections. The trail eventually turns back into a semblance of forest road, and spits you out in Unicoi State Park, where the most hardcore of you can branch off and do a couple of laps on the bike trail/race course. The rest of the ride is on pavement, taking you mostly downhill back to the bike shop. (Although I have

Hickory Nut Trail Loop

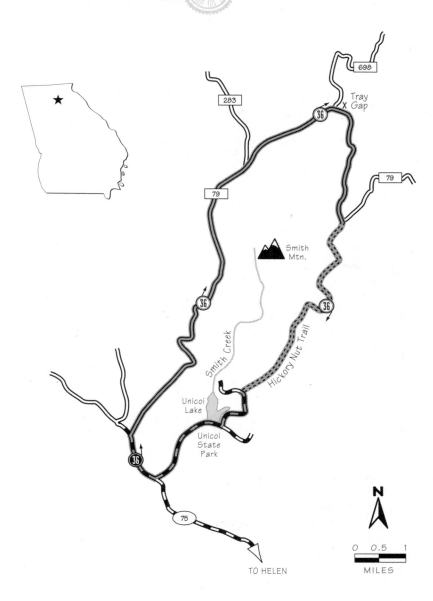

698

283

79

Tray
X Gap

36

79

Smith
Mtn.

36

36

Smith Creek

Hickory Nut Trail

Unicoi
Lake

Unicoi
State
Park

36

75

TO HELEN

N

0   0.5   1

MILES

avoided pavement rides like the plague, when you consider riding back up what you have just ridden down, even the most dirt-dedicated will agree that it's better to complete the loop this way.)

And, yes, someone will ride it backward, just because it's there. As a bonus, the scenery is spectacular on this ride, especially in the fall.

Restrictions: The listed forest roads are open to motorized traffic. Some sections of this loop are located within a wildlife management area, and are open to hunting during certain days of the year. The trails are closed during scheduled hunting days. Please check the bulletin boards at the trailhead, or call the number listed in Appendix C for information.

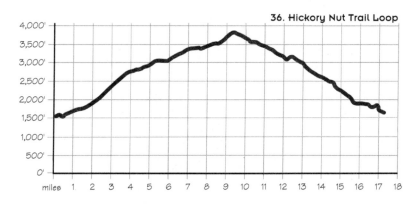

THE RIDE

0.0 From the parking area at the bike shop, continue along the paved road for 0.4 mile to the stop sign. Turn right at the stop sign and go 0.2 mile, then turn right on gravel Forest Road 79.

2.9 Waterfall.

3.1 Overlook to the right.

3.5 Unofficial camping area to the left.

3.6 Fenced area to the right.

6.6 FR 283 forks left to high shoals. Turn right on FR 79 to Tray Mountain.

8.5 Road forks at the Shallow Creek Wildlife Management Area sign. FR 698 goes to the left, and FR 79 goes right; go right. (The Appalachian Trail also crosses here; don't even think about riding a bike on the AT!)

9.6 Creek crossing. (Have you pedaled since the top?)

10.0 Camping area down to the left.

10.8 Overlook to the right (I think that's Helen down there).

11.0 T intersection; go straight across, around the dirt berm. The trail begins behind the berm, beyond a stretch of deadfall.

11.2 Rough section begins. Watch for various water bars and whoop-dee-doos at irregular intervals, along with a gazillion babyhead rocks.

13.8 The trail improves somewhat.

13.9 Trail forks with roadbeds to the left and right; go right, down the hill.

14.1 Scenic creek to the right.

15.4 Large waterfall. Just past the waterfall, the trail intersects with a hiking trail; go straight.

15.5 Trail intersects a paved road, GA 356. Turn left and follow GA 356 through Unicoi State Park.

16.3 Pass the cottages and lake to your right.

16.5 Pass a sign to Unicoi State Park.

16.8 Cross the dam on the paved road.

17.1 GA 356 leaves the park.

18.0 Turn right on the paved road at the Woody's Bike Shop sign. Ride ends at the bike shop. Thank Woody for the trail work.

Northeast Georgia

Northeast Georgia offers some excellent riding opportunities. Rabun County, near the North Carolina border, is laced with gravel Forest Service roads and county roads, and has plenty of trails to offer as well.

The Stonewall Loop is just a hint of some of the great riding in the area. Rabun County has its own SORBA chapter (these guys are everywhere), and the chapter members are one of the guiding forces to trail construction in the area, so look them up when you visit. They'll be happy to show you around, and just as happy to have you help out on one of their trail projects.

The Tallulah Gorge State Park bike trail is only a couple years old, and there are plans to add additional trails soon. Tallulah has also added a backcountry camping shelter down near the lake, so you can do an overnight bike trip in one of the few areas to offer such an option. The addition of other trails in the park will make it a destination in itself for rides.

The Lake Russell Wildlife Management Area is also covered with gravel forest roads, and other trails are planned for the area. There are several loop options around the Nancy Creek area, with the Ladyslipper Trail and Loop being a good example of the possibilities. The terrain around Lake Russell is not as rugged as Rabun County, but the rides are just as fun.

Stonewall Loop

Location:	Just outside the town of Tiger, about 6 miles north of Tallulah Falls, in Northeast Georgia.
Distance:	The loop described below is 6.8 miles.
Time:	1.5 hours.
Tread:	2 miles on singletrack, 1.6 miles on trail on old forest roadbed, and 3.2 miles on gated forest road.
Aerobic level:	Moderate.
Technical difficulty:	3.5.
Highlights:	Technical creek crossings, great views, new singletrack, excellent waterfalls.
Land status:	The trail is located in the Chattahoochee-Oconee National Forest, Tallulah District. This is a multi-use trail; please respect the rights of other users.

Stonewall Loop

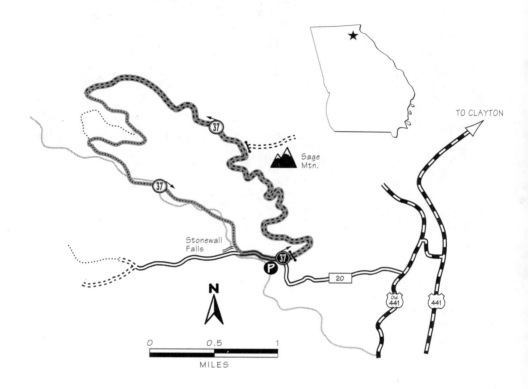

Maps:	USGS Tiger.
Access:	From Atlanta, go north on Interstate 85 to I-985; continue north on I-985. The road eventually becomes regular four lane and is signed as U.S. Highway 23/Georgia Highway 365. At Cornelia it becomes US 23/441. Continue north to Wiley, about 12 miles north of Tallulah Falls. Look for the BP gas station on your left and turn left onto old US 441. Go to the fourth road on your left, which is gravel Forest Road 20. Turn left and drive one mile until you see a gated road to your right. This is where the ride begins. Drive another 0.2 mile west on FR 20 to a parking area on the left.

Notes on the trail: The Stonewall Loop is one of my new favorites in northeastern Georgia. A classic example of a North Georgia trail, it incorporates gated forest road, grassy doubletrack, and freshly cut singletrack into a scenic up-and-down loop configuration with just enough technical challenge to keep you alert—a fun and interesting ride.

Scenery on the Stonewall Loop.

The initial climb on gravel forest road is cumbersome and tests your fitness, not because of the grade; but because of the loose gravel along the way that makes traction iffy at best. Even with my Clydesdale-seated weight over the rear wheel, it seemed like I was spinning halfway through each pedal stroke. Once you finally finish the climb though, you'll find a beautiful overlook that covers most of northern Rabun County. If you make the climb during the right season, you'll also find a nice little blueberry patch to take a break in while you admire the view. The fun begins from here; the ensuing downhill to the singletrack is fast and fun. The singletrack is its own reward, and Stonewall Falls is a great way to end any ride. Bring a camera and dry shoes because you will get wet on the creek crossings.

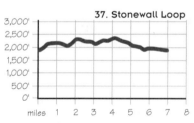

THE RIDE

0.0 From the parking area, travel 0.2 mile back along FR 20 to the gate on your left. Turn left.

0.4 Road forks; go left.

1.1 Connector trail enters from the left; go straight.

2.7 Blueberry patch overlook.

2.8 Trail forks; go left.

3.0 Trail forks; go left.

3.3 Singletrack begins.

4.2 Trail forks; go right (left is a shorter, steeper option).

4.4 Left fork rejoins the trail.

4.8 Fork in trail; go right (left is a steeper, more technical option).

5.1 Left fork rejoins the trail.

5.3 Trail rejoins an old roadbed. Another trail enters from the right; go straight.

5.5 Trail joins Stonewall Creek.

5.8 Creek crossing.

6.2 Creek crossing.

6.4 Creek crossing.

6.6 Creek crossing.

6.7 Connector trail enters from the left; go straight.

6.8 Trail ends at primitive camping area. Stonewall Falls is to your right.

Tallulah Gorge Trail

Location:	In Tallulah Falls, about 2 hours northeast of Atlanta.
Distance:	8.5 miles.
Time:	1.75 hours.
Tread:	8.5 miles on doubletrack forest roadbed.
Aerobic level:	Moderately easy.
Technical difficulty:	2.5.
Highlights:	Lake at the halfway point, views of the lake on the way down, awesome gorge nearby.
Land status:	The trail lies within Tallulah Gorge State Park.
Maps:	USGS Tugalo Lake.
Access:	From Atlanta, go north on Interstate 85 to I-985 north. Continue north as I-985 becomes U.S. Highway 23/441 at Cornelia. Stay on this four-lane highway 17 miles to the city of Tallulah Falls. The park entrance is just across the dam on the right. Follow the entrance road to the interpretive center and parking lot at the road's end. Park here.

Notes on the trail: Instead of an out-and-back, this is a down-and-up. The ride takes you from the interpretive center near the rim of Tallulah Gorge down old jeep roads to the shores of Tugalo Lake. The trail follows a gently graded series of old forest and jeep roads, winding through ever-changing ecosystems as you descend to the lake.

Tallulah Gorge Trail

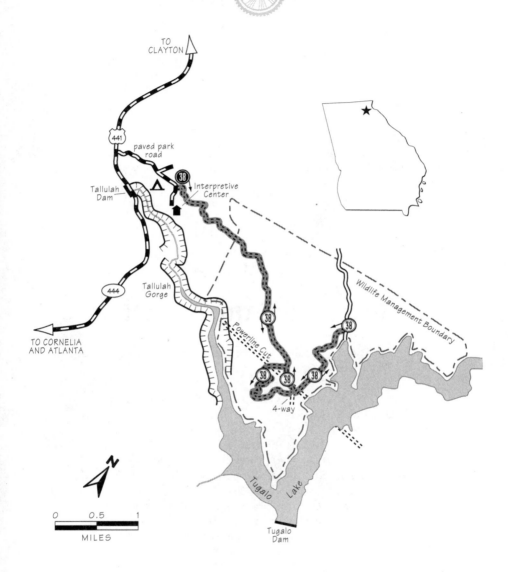

TO
CLAYTON

441

paved park
road

38

Interpretive
Center

Tallulah
Dam

Tallulah
Gorge

444

TO CORNELIA
AND ATLANTA

Powerline Cut

38

38

38

38

38

4-way

Wildlife Management Boundary

Tugalo   Lake

Tugalo
Dam

N

0   0.5   1

MILES

The lake at the halfway point makes a great spot for a summer cool-off. The water is cold, even on the hottest day, and a quick dip will invigorate you for the ride back up. The climb is relatively gentle.

Make sure to visit the Jane Hurt Yarn Interpretive Center before your ride; there are excellent displays of the local flora and fauna that you will experience on your ride, and a great historical perspective on the gorge.

Restrictions: Some sections of this trail are located within a wildlife management area, and the trails may be closed during scheduled hunting days. Please check at the interpretive center, or the trailhead, or call the number listed in Appendix C for information. You must purchase a $2 park pass to park in Georgia state parks.

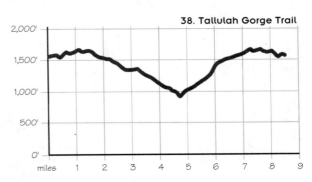

THE RIDE

0.0 From the parking lot pedal about 0.1 mile back up the entrance road to the trailhead on the right. The trail is blazed yellow.

0.6 Trail intersects a roadbed. Turn right, follow the roadbed for a short distance, then turn sharp left back off the roadbed.

1.0 Trail turns right at a gate; go right.

1.1 Trail crosses a powerline cut.

1.3 Roadbed forks; go left. Just ahead, another roadbed enters from the left; go straight.

1.4 Roadbed enters from the left; go straight. Large clearcut to the left.

1.6 Roadbed forks; go right.

1.7 Roadbed forks; go left.

1.9 Roadbed forks; go left.

2.1 Roadbed enters from the right; go straight.

2.3 Roadbed enters from the left; go straight.

2.4 Roadbed continues straight; trail goes right, around a gate. Turn right.

2.6 Roadbed crosses a powerline cut.

3.2 View of lake to the right.

3.5 Roadbed intersects another roadbed; go straight.

4.5 Roadbed enters from the right; turn right and go down the steep roadbed.

4.6 Roadbed intersects a gravel road; turn right on the gravel road.

4.7 Creek crossing; roadbed ends at a parking area just across the creek. This is the turnaround point. Take a break. To return, go back across the creek, up the road.

4.8 Turn left and go back up the steep roadbed to the left.

Getting ready to ride the Tallulah Gorge Trail.

5.7 Cross a powerline cut; overlook to the left.

5.8 Four-way intersection; turn right for a shorter climb. At the fork, go left, uphill.

5.9 Roadbed enters from the right rear; go left up the hill.

6.0 Cross the powerline cut.

6.1 Roadbed enters from the left rear; go straight.

6.2 The original trail enters from the left at the gate. Just ahead, another roadbed enters from the left; bear right.

6.3 Roadbed enters from the right; go straight.

6.5 Roadbed forks; go right.

6.6 Roadbed enters from the left rear; go straight.

6.8 Roadbed enters from the left rear; go straight.

7.0 Roadbed enters from the right rear; go straight.

7.1 Roadbed enters from the left rear; go straight.

7.2 Gated road enters from the right; go straight.

7.3 Trail enters from the left rear; go straight.

7.4 Cross the powerline cut.

7.5 Trail enters from the left; go left.

7.9 Turn sharp right onto a roadbed, then turn left just a few yards ahead at the fork.

8.5 Ride ends at the trailhead.

Ladyslipper Loop

Location:	4 miles east of Cornelia, about 1.5 hours from Atlanta.
Distance:	The loop described is 7.6 miles.
Time:	1.5 hours.
Tread:	0.6 mile on paved road, 1.8 miles on gravel forest and access roads, 0.8 mile on gated doubletrack, and 4.4 miles on singletrack on old roadbeds.
Aerobic level:	Moderate.
Technical difficulty:	3.5.
Highlights:	Lots of singletrack downhill, great whoop-dee-doos, nice view, good postride fishing spot.
Land status:	The trail lies within the Lake Russell Wildlife Management Area. This is a multi-use trail; please respect the rights of other users.
Maps:	USGS Ayersville, Lake Russell, and Baldwin.
Access:	From Atlanta, take Interstate 85 north to I-985 to the exit for Georgia Highway 197 Mt. Airy-Clarkesville.

Ladyslipper Loop

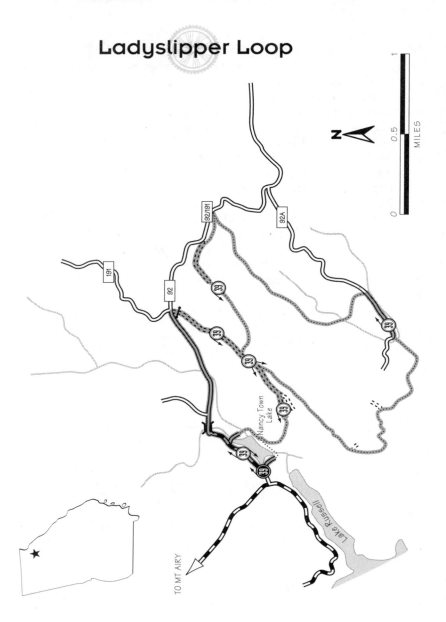

Turn right and go 2.6 miles to Dick's Hill Parkway. Turn right and travel 0.7 mile to Lake Russell Road, on the left. Turn left and drive 2 miles to an intersection; turn left toward the group camping area. The parking lot is at the right fork 0.1 mile ahead. To park here, purchase a pass for $3 at the gate just before the parking area.

Notes on the trail: The Ladyslipper Trail and Loop is a good mix of gravel forest road, doubletrack, and singletrack trail on old roadbeds. This loop configuration is a result of the experience of the locals in how to best ride the trail. The trail winds around in the forest east of Lake Russell, and gives riders a good taste of several different trail surfaces and conditions. There are several small stream crossings and a creek crossing, as well as a moderate climb on singletrack on old roadbed.

The trail is multi-use, and it shows. Some sections are eroded where the horse traffic has used one line, and at least one steep downhill section will probably be rerouted or reworked sometime soon. The news is not all bad though; the trail conditions offer some interesting technical challenges and keep you on your toes. Between the technical challenges and the rolling terrain, you will get a workout.

The water bars, dips, or whoop-dee-doos are irresistible on two of the downhill sections, and even I got some good air on a few. There is a nice view of the eastern foothills from the high point of the ride.

The lake offers swimming and fishing for a good postride cool-down, and there are many other gravel forest road loop opportunities in the area. It's a great place to spend a day.

Restrictions: Some sections of this trail are located within a wildlife management area, and are open to hunting during certain days of the year. The trails may be closed during scheduled hunting days. Please check at the trailhead, or call the number listed in Appendix C for information.

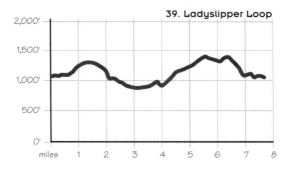

39. Ladyslipper Loop

THE RIDE

0.0 From the parking area, ride around the gate and along the road next to the lake past the picnic area. On the other side of the lake is another parking lot; a sign there points to the Ladyslipper Trailhead to the right. Continue straight past this parking area and trailhead, along the paved road.

0.4 Turn right and cross a bridge; the road turns to gravel.

0.5 Road enters from the left; stay straight.

0.8 Cross a bridge; nice waterfall to the left.

1.3 T intersection with gravel Forest Road 191; from the right rear is another gated road. Go around the gate and follow this roadbed back to the right.

1.7 Ladyslipper Trail enters from left. Do not go left. Stay on the gravel roadbed.

1.8 Second trailhead to the left; Nancytown Trail sign points ahead. Go left. (The trail is marked with blue blazes.)

2.0 Roadbed enters from the left; bear right.

2.3 Trail forks; go right, down a steep section.

2.4 Sharp switchback right onto another roadbed.

2.6 Stream crossing.

3.0 Trail enters a clearing.

3.2 Trail enters another clearing.

3.4 Trail crosses a creek; just across is a T intersection with a gravel forest road. Turn right on the forest road.

4.0 Trail enters from the left at blue blazes; turn left back onto the trail.

4.2 Trail turns right and crosses a footbridge over a creek.

4.3 Trail turns left and crosses another footbridge.

5.2 Trail turns sharp left at FR 191; turn left and follow the trail parallel to the road.

5.4 Trail intersects with a gravel forest road, then immediately forks left up a steep hill on another roadbed; go left up the hill.

5.6 View to the left.

6.1 Trail intersects with doubletrack (you passed this way earlier); turn left on the doubletrack.

6.2 Pass the second trailhead you turned left on earlier; stay on the doubletrack.

6.5 Trail forks right from roadbed; go right.

7.1 Trail forks by a stone picnic shelter; go right and cross a stream.

7.2 Stream crossing.

7.25 Cross a bridge and enter the parking lot at the picnic area you passed earlier. Go out of the parking lot and turn left, following the road back past the gate and to the parking lot.

7.6 Ride ends at the parking lot.

Gainesville (Chicopee Woods)

In 1995, longtime SORBA members Tom and Belinda Sauret began exploring the possibility of using property owned by the Chicopee Woods Area Park Commission for mountain bike trails. The land is held in trust for the recreational use of the local residents. A popular golf course already made good use of some of the land, and course expansions were planned. The Elatchee Nature Center used a more isolated tract across the interstate. The section between the two was not being used for much of anything, so the Saurets, being visionaries, approached the commissioners with their idea. They met with some initial resistance, but persistence paid, and today's trail system is a tribute to their tenacity.

With the help of local riders, bike shops, and SORBA, the Outer Loop was constructed using mostly existing roadbeds and trails. The Inner Loop and Lake Loop soon followed.

The bridges, switchbacks, crossings, signage, and almost everything else was donated free of charge and built by volunteers. Enjoy the trails, and when you come up to ride, check the bulletin board for dates of work parties. The SORBA Gainesville chapter usually provides lunch, and you'll enjoy working with the regulars. Remember, everything here is built and maintained by volunteers. Please respect the efforts of those who put so much into making Chicopee a local favorite, and take some time to help out.

The Gainesville College Trail is the result of the cooperation of several groups, including the Gainesville College Foundation, the Gainesville College Students for Environmental Awareness and the Science Division, and the Gainesville-SORBA chapter. The trail was officially opened in October 1997, with an inaugural race and festival, and much fanfare from the local riding community. The existence of the trail is a tribute to cooperation between different groups; the excellent bridges were built courtesy of the science club, whose members also surveyed the trail for mapping. The majority of the labor to construct and maintain the trail was and is provided by SORBA volunteers and other members of the local riding community. The two local bike shops contributed manpower, promotion, and prizes to help make this trail a reality. And the Gainesville College Foundation was open-minded enough to allow a new use for some of the college property. If fact, plans to sell some of the property may be reexamined because of the popularity of the bike trail. There are plans to connect the Gainesville College Trail with the trails at Chicopee Woods, just a few miles from the campus.

Walnut Creek Outer Loop

Location:	In Gainesville, about 45 minutes north of Atlanta.
Distance:	5.5 miles.
Time:	1.25 hours.
Tread:	0.6 mile on gravel road, 1 mile on doubletrack, and 3.9 miles on singletrack, some on old roadbed.
Aerobic level:	Moderately easy.
Technical difficulty:	2.5.
Highlights:	Great buffed singletrack, proximity to civilization, many ride options.
Land status:	The trail is on property owned by the city of Gainesville.
Maps:	USGS Gainesville.
Access:	From Atlanta, go north on Interstate 85/Interstate 985 to Exit 4 for Georgia Highway 53. Turn left off the exit ramp on GA 53. Just after you go under the bridge, turn right on the frontage road and follow it for 0.7 mile until it meets GA 13. Go left on GA 13 and follow it for 1.4 miles, to Chicopee Village, on the right. Turn right, then immediately right again on Elatchee Drive, at the sign to the Elatchee Nature Center. Follow Elatchee Drive past the golf course to the gated bike parking area to the left.

Notes on the trail: The Outer Loop uses existing roadbed and fixtures combined with newly cut singletrack to make a 5.5-mile loop ride. This trail shares much of its length with the Inner Loop, but adds almost a mile of new singletrack to the experience. Once you get to the other end of the property from the parking area, there's a stretch of singletrack that was obviously made by and for mountain bikers. Follow this and relish the apparent isolation of being in the woods away from everything (by the way, just over that hill is I-985). In the winter, the isolation is not as apparent, because you can hear traffic in the distance.

The bridges and switchbacks and the extensive sidehill construction all combine to create a great riding experience, and are a testament to the dedication and tenacity of those volunteers who have made all of this possible.

Restrictions: The trails are closed during wet weather and during some maintenance days. For trail status, call the SORBA trail information hotline

Walnut Creek
Inner & Outer Loops

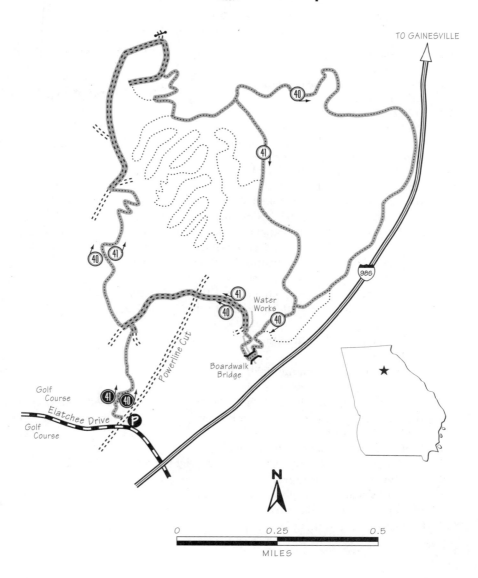

TO GAINESVILLE

Water Works

Boardwalk Bridge

Powerline Cut

Golf Course

Elatchee Drive

Golf Course

N

| 0 | 0.25 | 0.5 |

MILES

at 770-297-8319. Please respect the closure policy; if the parking lot gate is closed and you park along the road, you will get a ticket.

THE RIDE

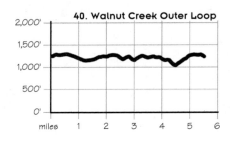

40. Walnut Creek Outer Loop

0.0 From the parking lot, ride back along the entrance driveway to the trail, which goes across the powerline cut and into the woods.

0.1 Trail crosses a roadbed.

0.4 Trail intersects with a gravel roadbed. Turn left on the gravel road, then immediately turn right, back into the woods. Follow the sign to Rocky Way.

0.9 Trail forks; go left.

1.1 Trail intersects a gravel roadbed; turn right.

1.2 Trail forks to the right; stay left on the gravel roadbed.

1.3 Road forks; go right. The gravel road is following a powerline cut and a creek.

1.7 Gate across gravel road ahead; turn right.

1.8 Trail turns left off the roadbed; go left. Singletrack begins.

1.9 Trail enters from the right; go left.

2.0 Trail intersection; go left (to the right is the Zig-Zag Trail).

2.3 Trail intersection; turn left (to the right is the Inner Loop).

3.0 Cross a bridge.

3.3 I-985 is just over the hill to the left. Feels isolated, doesn't it?

4.0 Trail forks; go right.

4.1 Inner Loop enters from the right; go left.

4.3 Trail enters from the left; go straight.

4.4 Trail turns sharp left, down the hill. The trail ahead is a closed trail. Go left.

4.5 Trail crosses a bridge on the powerline cut. Turn right across the bridge, into the bamboo forest.

4.5 Trail crosses a creek on a stone trailbed.

4.6 Creek crossing. Just across the creek, turn right on the gravel road.

5.0 Trail turns left off the gravel road; go left.

5.1 Trail forks right off the old roadbed; go right.

5.4 Trail crosses the old roadbed.

5.5 Ride ends at the parking lot.

Walnut Creek Inner Loop

See Map
on Page 139

Location: In Gainesville, about 45 minutes north of Atlanta.

Distance: 4.7 miles.

Time: 1 hour.

Tread: 1 mile on gravel road, 0.6 mile on doubletrack, and 3.1 miles on singletrack, some on old roadbed.

Aerobic level: Moderate.

Technical difficulty: 2.5.

Highlights: Great singletrack, other loops close by, creek crossings, close to civilization.

Land status: The trail is located on property owned by the city of Gainesville.

Maps: USGS Gainesville.

Access: From Atlanta, go north on Interstate 85 and Interstate 985 to Exit 4 for Georgia Highway 53. Turn left off the exit ramp on GA 53. Just after you go under the bridge, turn right on the frontage road. Follow the frontage road 0.7 mile until it meets GA 13. Go left on GA 13 and follow it for 1.4 miles, to Chicopee Village, on the right. Turn right, then immediately right again on Elatchee Drive, at the sign to the Elatchee Nature Center. Follow Elatchee Drive past the golf course to the gated bike parking area to the left.

Notes on the trail: The Inner Loop is a shorter—but no easier—option to the Outer Loop. The loop shares much of its length with the Outer Loop, though it never nears the interstate. There is less singletrack, but what's there is a challenge and great fun to ride. Take a lap around the Inner Loop, then do the Outer Loop for more distance. The creek crossings will cool you off in summer, and the gravel road climb will warm you up in winter. The scenery changes with the seasons, and there are some nice spots to stop and ponder the meaning of life. Most folks don't though, because they're having too much fun riding the trails here.

Restrictions: The trails are closed during wet weather and during some maintenance days. For trail status, call the SORBA trail info hotline at 770-297-8319. Please respect the closure policy; if the parking lot gate is closed and you park along the road, you will get a ticket.

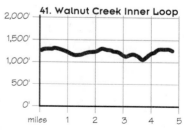

THE RIDE

0.0 From the parking lot, ride back along the entrance driveway to the trail, which goes across the powerline cut and into the woods.

0.1 Trail crosses a roadbed.

0.4 Trail intersects with a gravel roadbed. Turn left on the gravel road, then immediately turn right, back into the woods. Follow the sign to Rocky Way.

0.9 Trail forks; go left.

1.1 Trail intersects a gravel roadbed; turn right.

1.2 Trail forks to the right; stay left on the gravel roadbed.

1.3 Road forks; go right. The gravel road is following a powerline cut and a creek.

1.7 Gate across the gravel road ahead; turn right.

1.8 Trail turns left off the roadbed; go left. Singletrack begins.

1.9 Trail enters from the right; go left.

2.0 Trail intersection; go left. (To the right is the Zig-Zag Trail.)

2.3 Trail intersection; go right. The trail follows an old roadbed.

2.7 Trail leaves the roadbed.

3.0 Cross the bridge over a creek and turn left.

3.2 Outer Loop enters from the left; go right.

3.4 Trail enters from the left; go straight.

3.5 Trail turns sharp left, down the hill. The trail ahead is closed. Go left.

3.6 Trail crosses a bridge on the powerline cut. Turn right across the bridge, into the bamboo forest.

3.6 Trail crosses a creek on a stone trailbed.

3.7 Creek crossing. Just across the creek, turn right on the gravel road.

4.1 Trail turns left off the gravel road; go left.

4.2 Trail forks right off the old roadbed; go right.

4.6 Trail crosses the old roadbed.

4.7 Ride ends at the parking lot.

Zig-Zag Loop

Location:	In Gainesville, about 45 minutes north of Atlanta.
Distance:	7.6 miles.
Time:	1.5 hours.
Tread:	1 mile on gravel road and 6.6 miles on singletrack, some on old roadbeds.
Aerobic level:	Moderate.
Technical difficulty:	3.5.
Highlights:	Twisty singletrack, lots of singletrack, and more singletrack.
Land status:	The trail is located on property owned by the city of Gainesville.
Maps:	USGS Gainesville.
Access:	From Atlanta, go north on Interstate 85/Interstate 985 to Exit 4 for Georgia Highway 53. Turn left off the exit ramp on GA 53. Just after you go under the bridge, turn right onto the frontage road; which you follow for 0.7 mile until it meets GA 13. Go left on GA 13 and follow it for 1.4 miles, to Chicopee Village, on the right. Turn right, then immediately right again on Elatchee Drive, at the sign to the Elatchee Nature Center. Follow Elatchee Drive past the golf course to the gated bike parking area to the left.

Notes on the trail: If you love tight, twisty singletrack, then you'll love the Zig-Zag Loop. Using the connector trail and part of the Inner Loop, the ride is 7.6 miles of mostly singletrack heaven.

The trail actually runs inside of the Inner Loop, but takes full advantage of the terrain and density of the woods to give you a twisting, turning, switchback fest of great riding. The trails are narrow, and most are true singletrack, without the benefit of an old roadbed for wider passage. One section makes you think twice about bar ends because as the trees are so close you have to do a little jiggle to get through.

The volunteers at Chicopee have done it again with their latest addition to the trail system. The Zig-Zag Loop proves it does get even better.

Restrictions: The trails are closed during wet weather and some maintenance days. For trail status, call the SORBA trail information hotline at 770-297-8319. Please respect the closure policy; if the parking lot gate is closed and you park along the road, you will get a ticket.

Zig-Zag Loop

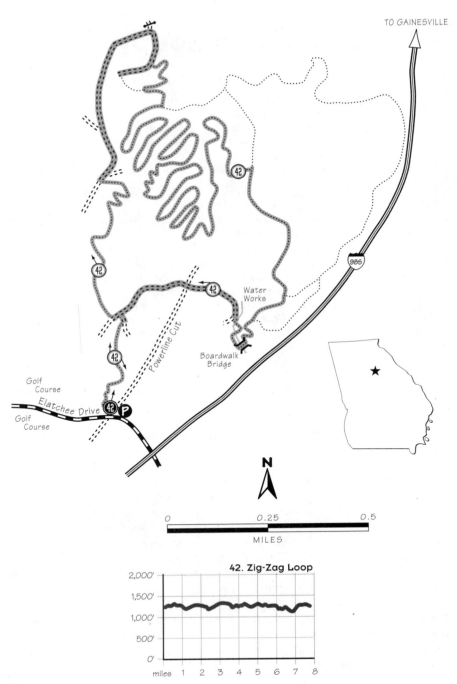

TO GAINESVILLE

42

986

Water
Works

Powerline Cut

42

42

42

Boardwalk
Bridge

Golf
Course

Elatchee Drive

42 P

Golf
Course

N

| 0 | 0.25 | 0.5 |

MILES

42. Zig-Zag Loop

2,000'

1,500'

1,000'

500'

0'

miles 1 2 3 4 5 6 7 8

THE RIDE

0.0 From the parking lot, ride back along the entrance driveway to the trail, which goes across the powerline cut and into the woods.

0.1 Trail crosses a roadbed.

0.4 Trail intersects with a gravel roadbed. Turn left on the gravel road, then immediately turn right, back into the woods. Follow the sign to Rocky Way.

0.9 Trail forks; go left.

1.1 Trail intersects a gravel roadbed; turn right.

1.2 Trail forks to the right; stay left on the gravel roadbed.

1.3 Road forks; go right. The gravel follows a powerline cut and a creek.

1.7 Gate across a gravel road ahead; turn right.

1.8 Trail turns left off the roadbed; go left. Singletrack begins.

1.9 Trail enters from the right; turn left.

2.0 Trail intersection; turn right (to the left are the Inner and Outer loops).

3.5 Switchback city!

5.8 Train intersection; turn right and join the Inner Loop.

5.9 Cross a footbridge.

6.2 Trail intersection; go right.

6.5 Switchback onto the powerline cut, then cross a bridge. Turn right just across the bridge.

6.6 Creek crossing. Just ahead is another creek crossing, then a steep bank up to the gravel roadbed. Turn right on the gravel roadbed.

6.9 Gravel roadbed crosses the powerline cut.

7.1 Trail turns left off the gravel roadbed; turn left.

7.5 Trail crosses a roadbed; go straight.

7.6 Ride ends at the parking lot.

The Lake Loop

Location:	In Gainesville, about 45 minutes north of Atlanta.
Distance:	2.6 miles.
Time:	45 minutes.
Tread:	2.4 miles on singletrack, some on old roadbed; 0.2 mile on paved road.
Aerobic level:	Moderately easy.
Technical difficulty:	1.5.
Highlights:	A pleasant little trail that runs around a lake bordering the golf course. Makes a nice addition to the other loops at Chicopee.
Land status:	The trail is located in Chicopee Woods, a tract of land owned by the city of Gainesville.
Maps:	USGS Chestnut Mountain.
Access:	From Atlanta, go north on Interstate 85/Interstate 985 to Exit 4 for Georgia Highway 53. Turn left off the exit ramp on GA 53. Just after you go under the bridge, turn right onto the frontage road, which you follow for 0.7 mile until it meets GA 13. Go left on GA 13 and follow it for 1.4 miles, to Chicopee Village, on the right. Turn right, then immediately right again on Elatchee Drive, at the sign to the Elatchee Nature Center. Follow Elatchee Drive past the golf course to the gated bike parking area to the left.

Notes on the trail: The Lake Loop is a nice little diversion from the other longer and more difficult loops at Chicopee Woods. The trail winds down by a lake, and some sections border the golf course (you can't really tell because of the dense woods and undergrowth). Consisting mostly of singletrack and some old roadbeds, the trail has just enough twists and turns to keep your attention. A couple of short winding climbs will get your heart rate up, and the rooty sections will hone your woods-riding skills. Until you break onto the powerline cut, it's easy to forget just how close to everything you really are. If you've got some time and a newer rider, take them on this trail for some fun skills training.

Restrictions: The trails are closed during wet weather and some maintenance days. For trail status, call the SORBA trail info hotline at 770-297-8319. Please respect the closure policy; if the parking lot gated is closed and you park along the road, you will get a ticket.

The Lake Loop

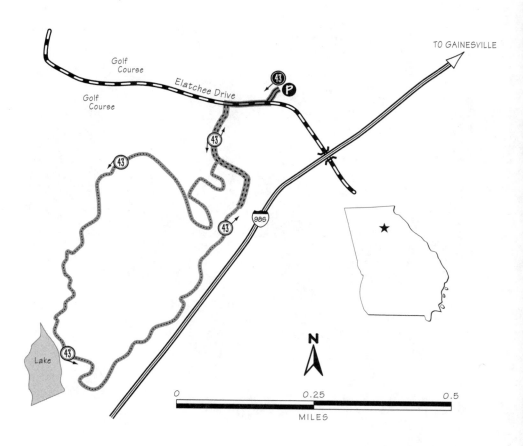

THE RIDE

0.0 From the parking lot on Elatchee Drive, go back along the paved road toward the golf course.

0.1 Turn left through a gate and down a dirt roadbed.

0.5 Roadbed turns into a singletrack.

1.0 Trail runs along the lake.

1.3 Cross a small bridge.

1.4 Trail joins an old roadbed; follow the trail right.

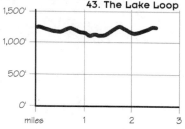

Alfred Barker rides Chicopee Woods.

1.7 Trail enters powerline cut and immediately re-enters the woods.
2.1 Creek crossing.
2.3 Trail intersects with an old roadbed; turn left.
2.4 Trail enters powerline cut.
2.5 Intersection with Elatchee Drive; turn right to return to the parking lot.
2.6 Ride ends at the parking lot.

Gainesville College Bike Trail

Location:	In Oakwood, about 40 minutes northeast of Atlanta.
Distance:	3.3 miles.
Time:	45 minutes.
Tread:	3.3 miles on singletrack, some on old roadbed.
Aerobic level:	Easy.
Technical difficulty:	2. The trail is tight and twisty in some sections.
Highlights:	Easy to find and convenient, an excellent beginner practice loop.
Land status:	The trail is on the private property of Gainesville College.
Maps:	USGS Chestnut Mountain.
Access:	From Atlanta, go north on Interstate 85 to Interstate 985. Get off at Exit 4 for Oakwood, and turn left. Gainesville College is about 0.3 mile on the right. Take the second entrance, and follow to the parking lot just past the athletic building, which overlooks the facilities building. The trailhead is at the edge of the woods toward the rear of the property.

Notes on the trail: The Gainesville College Trail offers a lot of narrow singletrack that twists and turns through the woods around some old farm ruins and hardwood forests. Though narrow, the trail is great for beginners and less confident riders because of the lack of much climbing. My wife and I rode the trail with our sons in child seats on the back of the bikes; AJ actually went to sleep during the ride! Our eight-year-old daughter Stephanie had no trouble following along on her own. If you want to introduce someone to mountain biking but don't have time a lot of time, this is a great trail.

Gainesville College Bike Trail

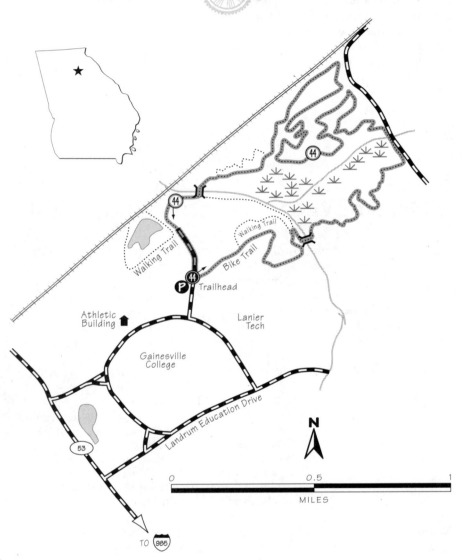

The Gainesville College Bike Trail.

Restrictions: The trail is closed during wet weather and some maintenance days. For trail status, call the SORBA trail information hotline at 770-297-8319. Please respect the closure policy.

THE RIDE

0.0 From the parking lot, follow the path to the trailhead at the edge of the woods. Cross a small footbridge and the singletrack starts.

0.5 Trail enters a cleared powerline right-of-way. Turn right and go about 100 yards, then turn left and cross a large wooden bridge.

0.6 Trail re-enters the woods.

1.2 Trail leaves the woods at a paved street. Turn left and ride along the edge of the street about 150 yards, past the wetland area on the left. The trail re-enters the woods to the left.

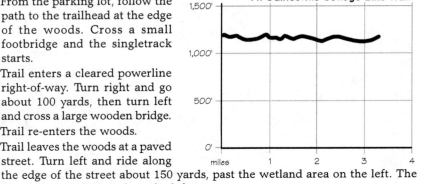

1.7 Trail forks; go left.

2.0 Trail enters from the left; go straight.

2.1 Cross a small footbridge over a stream.

2.2 Pass an abandoned well on the right.

2.6 Enter a cleared powerline right-of-way and turn left.

2.7 Trail forks; go right back into the woods.

2.9 Cross a small bridge.

3.0 Trail re-enters the cleared powerline right-of-way; turn right and cross the bridge.

3.1 Trail forks; go left on a gravel roadbed behind the maintenance shed. At the next fork, go right, along the edge of the pond to the paved road.

3.3 Ride ends (or second lap begins) at the parking lot.

Mistletoe State Park
(Augusta Area)

If you're a mountain bike neophyte, or looking for a place to bring beginners and children to introduce them to mountain biking, here it is. The trails in the park are all flat and easy. The shorter trails give you plenty of choices for ride lengths. The trails run through pine forests along gentle slopes through what used to be farmland; you can still see the terraces in places. The woods are nearly free of heavy undergrowth, so wildlife spotting is almost guaranteed. I saw many deer here while doing these maps, and sign of many more. The trails are easy for the most part, though some of the footbridges were built for foot traffic and have difficult approaches. There are few steep hills and no long climbs.

The park itself is on the shores of Clarks Hill Lake, a large manmade lake that sits on the border of Georgia and South Carolina. The park offers a beach, playgrounds, picnic areas, boat ramps, 102 campsites with water and electrical hookups, and ten two-bedroom cottages that sleep up to eight. I took the family along for the weekend while mapping these trails, and we thoroughly enjoyed the cottage and facilities. My eight-year-old daughter rode some of the trails, and had no problem with them.

The use of mountain bikes on the park's trails is a relatively new idea. Keep that in mind when you encounter other users. The current park management is very open to providing user facilities for bike riders, if we do our part and help build and maintain the trails, and conduct ourselves courteously around other trail users. There is at least one other trail planned in the park.

The proximity of the Keg Creek Loop to the park gives beginning riders a series of four trails of progressively more difficult levels to experience, all within a small area and close to some excellent overnight facilities. For reservations and park information, see Appendix C in the back of this book.

Twin Oaks Loop

Location:	About 28 miles northwest of Augusta, 8 miles north of Interstate 20, about 2.5 hours from Atlanta.
Distance:	4 miles.
Time:	45 minutes.
Tread:	3.8 miles on singletrack and 0.2 mile on paved park road.
Aerobic level:	Easy.
Technical difficulty:	1.5. (The footbridges are tricky!)
Highlights:	Easy beginner trail through flat pine woods, beach at the start/finish, lots of wildlife.
Land status:	The trail lies within Mistletoe State Park. This is a multi-use connector trail for park guests; please respect the rights of other users.
Maps:	USGS Appling.
Access:	From Atlanta, go east on Interstate 20 to Exit 60 for Georgia Highway 150. Go left 3.4 miles on GA 150, turn left on Mistletoe Road, and go 2.9 miles to the park entrance. Just inside the park entrance, turn left and go 0.4 mile. Turn right at the office sign and travel 0.9 mile to the beach area parking lot. Park here; the trailhead is on the opposite side of the parking lot from the office.

Notes on the trail: The Twin Oaks Trail is a connector that takes you from the beach area past a section of the lake, to the campground along the lake, then past a series of wildlife viewing areas, and back to the beach. If you're looking for a good first ride for yourself or someone you're introducing to mountain biking, this is a great trail. You can do one loop, then try one of the more difficult park trails, or take a refreshing dip at the beach, or both. The trail is very well marked and easy to follow. Other than the footbridges, the trail is free of obstacles.

Restrictions: A Georgia park pass is required for parking in Georgia state parks.

Twin Oaks Loop •
Cliatt Creek Loop

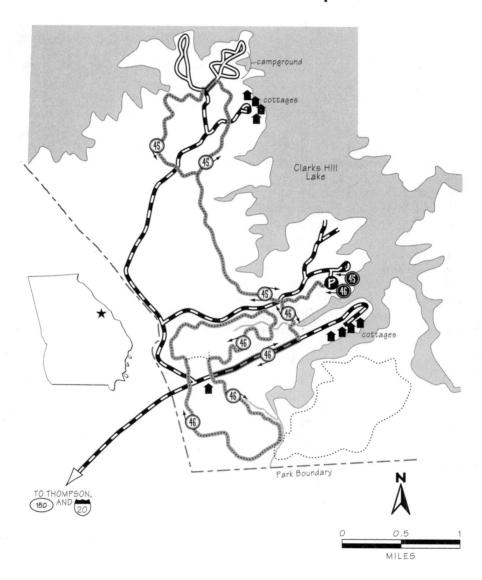

campground

cottages

Clarks Hill
Lake

45

45

P
45
46
46

46
cottages

46
46

46

Park Boundary

TO THOMPSON,
150 AND 20

N

0   0.5   1
MILES

THE RIDE

0.0 The trailhead is on the edge of the woods, directly across the parking lot from the beach office. You will immediately cross a footbridge.

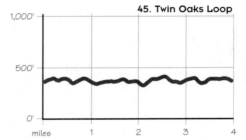

0.2 Trail intersects with the Cottage Trail; turn right and cross the paved road. The trail is blazed yellow.

0.5 Cross a footbridge.

0.7 Cross a footbridge.

0.8 Trail turns right and joins an old roadbed.

0.9 Trail turns left and leaves the roadbed.

1.0 Cross a footbridge.

1.1 Cross two footbridges close together.

1.2 Trail intersection; go right and follow the yellow and white blazes.

1.6 Trail intersects a paved park road; go straight across.

1.8 Trail intersects another paved park road; turn left and follow the paved road.

1.9 A paved road enters from the right. Just across this road, the trail re-enters the woods. This section of the trail is blazed white.

2.1 Cross a footbridge. The lake is to your right.

2.5 Trail passes a large wildlife viewing area to the right.

2.6 Trail intersects a paved park road; go straight across, past the wildlife viewing area.

2.8 Trail intersection; go right and follow the yellow blazes. (Go left for another loop.)

2.9 Cross a footbridge.

3.0 Cross two footbridges close together.

3.1 Trail turns right and joins an old roadbed.

3.2 Trail turns left and leaves an old roadbed.

3.3 Cross a footbridge.

3.5 Cross a footbridge.

3.6 Trail intersects a paved park road; cross the road and turn left at the intersection with the Cottage Trail.

4.0 Cross a footbridge. Ride ends at the parking lot.

Cliatt Creek Loop

See Map on Page 155

Location: 28 miles northwest of Augusta, about 2.5 hours from Atlanta.

Distance: 4.3 miles.

Time: 1 hour.

Tread: 3.5 miles on singletrack and 0.8 mile on paved park road.

Aerobic level: Easy.

Technical difficulty: 1.5. (The footbridges are tricky!)

Highlights: Nice section along the creek, a little more challenge than the Beach/Campground Trail, abundant wildlife.

Land status: The trail lies within Mistletoe State Park. This is a multi-use trail; please respect the rights of other users.

Maps: USGS Appling.

Access: From Atlanta, go east on Interstate 20 to Exit 60 for Georgia Highway 150. Go left 3.4 miles on GA 150, turn left on Mistletoe Road, and drive 2.9 miles to the park entrance. Just inside the park entrance, turn left and go 0.4 mile. Turn right at the office sign and travel 0.9 mile to the beach area parking lot. Park here; the trailhead is on the opposite side of the parking lot from the office.

Notes on the trail: So you've done the Twin Oaks Trail and you're ready for a little more challenge. Try this one. The grades are a little steeper, and there are a few more obstacles.

The footbridges at most of the water crossings are wide enough for bikes, although the approaches are difficult. Most sections feel remote and are quiet (except for the muttering and cursing caused by some trying to ride some of the footbridges).

This trail meanders through several mini-ecosystems, with abundant wildlife and plenty of convenient viewing areas. Part of the trail follows Cliatt Creek through a hardwood forest as it flows toward the lake. Another section wanders through a thick piny woods with a gentle series of dips and rolls, taking advantage of the natural gentle contours of the land. The hardwood forest is in the lesser-used section of the park, and feels even more isolated.

Restrictions: A Georgia park pass is required for parking in all Georgia state parks.

0.0 The trailhead is on the edge of the woods, directly across the parking lot from the beach office. You will immediately cross a footbridge.

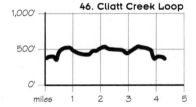

0.2 Trail intersects with the Cottage Trail; go left on the Cottage Trail.

0.4 Cross a footbridge at the bottom of a deep gully. The steep section up the other side is a pusher for almost everyone.

0.5 Intersection with a paved park road; turn right and ride along the road.

0.9 Trailhead is to the left just before the ranger's residence. Go left down the trail.

1.4 Trail turns left and follows the creek.

1.5 Small waterfall.

1.7 Trail enters a clearing.

1.8 Trail passes a larger clearing to the left.

2.1 Trail intersects a paved park road; go straight across and look for white blazes.

2.2 Trail intersects another paved park road; go straight across and look for the yellow and white blazes to the left of the nature center.

2.3 Trail intersection; go left and follow the yellow blazes (to the right is a shortcut).

2.4 Cross a footbridge; wildlife viewing area is to the left.

2.7 Cross a footbridge.

2.9 Cross a footbridge.

3.0 Cross a footbridge.

3.1 Cross a footbridge.

3.3 Trail intersection; go left, cross a footbridge.

3.4 Trail intersects paved park road across from the ranger's residence; turn left and follow the paved park road.

3.8 Trailhead to the left; go left, down a steep hill.

3.9 Cross a footbridge.

4.1 Intersection with Beach/Campground Trail; go right.

4.3 Cross a footbridge. Ride ends at the parking lot.

Rock Dam Loop

Location:	28 miles northwest of Augusta, about 2.5 hours from Atlanta.
Distance:	6.4 miles.
Time:	1.5 hours.
Tread:	0.8 mile on paved park road, and 5.6 miles on singletrack trail, some on old roadbed.
Aerobic level:	Moderately easy.
Technical difficulty:	2.5.
Highlights:	Creek crossings, waterfalls, lake views, lots of wildlife.
Land status:	The trail lies within Mistletoe State Park. This is a multi-use trail; please respect the rights of other users.
Maps:	USGS Appling.
Access:	From Atlanta, go east on Interstate 20 to Exit 60 for Georgia Highway 150. Go left 3.4 miles on GA 150, turn left on Mistletoe Road, and drive 2.9 miles to the park entrance. Just inside the park entrance, turn left and go 0.4 mile. Turn right at the office sign and travel 0.9 mile to the beach area parking lot. Park here; the trailhead is on the opposite side of the parking lot from the office.

Notes on the trail: Okay, so now you've ridden the Twin Oaks Trail, moved on to the Cliatt Creek Trail, and are ready for more of a challenge. Well, here it is.

This version of the Rock Dam Loop incorporates part of the Cliatt Creek Trail to create a figure eight for more distance. The Rock Dam section is farther back in the unused area of the park, and the trail is less used and more technical. This section is very new (it had just been flagged when I mapped it), and will take a couple of years to wear in. This description may differ some from the final result, after the usual route tweaking that is always a part of a new trail. Another section across the creek at Rock Dam is planned, but it was not ready at this writing. Use common sense on some sections; there's nothing too technical here, but some of the unbridged creek crossings are slick and tricky. Logs across the trail, creek crossings, a mud bog, a rocky sidehill, and more elevation change will keep you interested for the entire ride.

Restrictions: A Georgia park pass is required for parking in all Georgia state parks.

Rock Dam Loop

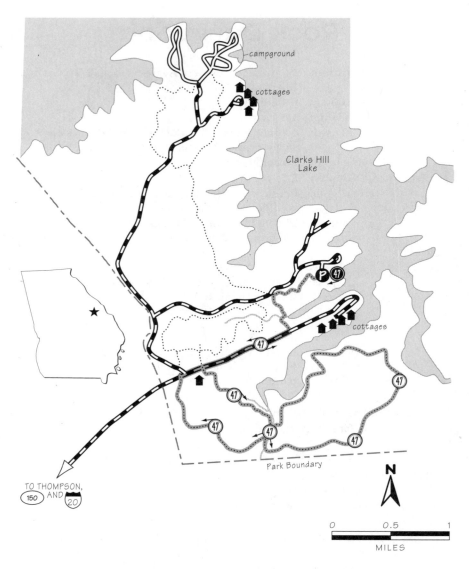

campground

cottages

Clarks Hill Lake

P 47

cottages

47

47

47

47

47

Park Boundary

N

TO THOMPSON, 150 AND 20

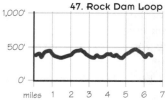

0   0.5   1

MILES

47. Rock Dam Loop

1,000'

500'

0'

miles 1 2 3 4 5 6 7

THE RIDE

0.0 The trailhead is on the edge of the woods, directly across the parking lot from the beach office. You will immediately cross a footbridge.

0.2 Trail intersects with the Cottage Trail; go left on the Cottage Trail.

0.4 Cross a footbridge at the bottom of a deep gully. The steep section up the other side is a pusher for almost everyone.

0.5 Intersection with a paved park road; turn right and ride along the road.

0.9 Trailhead is to the left just before the ranger's residence. Go left down the trail.

1.4 Trail turns and follows the creek.

1.5 Small waterfall.

1.6 Trail intersection. There is a small post marked with an "I." Go left.

1.7 Creek crossing.

2.1 Cross a footbridge.

2.3 Trail intersects an old roadbed; go right.

2.4 Mud bog.

2.5 Trail turns left and leaves the roadbed, then joins another.

2.8 Trail turns right and leaves the roadbed.

2.9 Creek crossing; the lake is to your right.

3.0 Cross a footbridge, then turn right and ride down a dry wash.

3.1 Trail follows a creek.

3.2 Rock Dam (aptly named). The trail continues along this side of the creek to the left. (Another loop may cross the creek here in the future.)

3.4 Trail leaves the creek and turns left up a hill.

3.6 Cross a footbridge.

3.8 Rocky section.

4.1 Trail intersects a woods road; go straight across.

4.6 Another rocky section. The lake is to your right.

4.7 Trail crosses a creek and rejoins the Nature Trail. Go left on the Nature Trail.

4.9 Loop trail intersects from left with a small "I" marker; go left to do another loop or go straight to finish the ride.

5.2 Trail enters a clearing.

5.5 Trail intersects with a paved park road; turn right and ride the road that passes the ranger's residence.

5.9 Cottage Trail to the left; turn left.

6.0 Cross a footbridge at the bottom of a steep hill.

6.2 Trail intersects with Beach/Campground Trail to the left; go straight.

6.4 Cross a footbridge. Ride ends at the parking lot.

48

Keg Creek Loop

Location:	22 miles northwest of Augusta, about 2.5 hours east of Atlanta.
Distance:	7.9 miles.
Time:	1.5 hours.
Tread:	7.4 miles on singletrack, and 0.5 mile on paved road.
Aerobic level:	Easy.
Technical difficulty:	2.5.
Highlights:	Trail follows a section of shoreline of Clarks Hill Lake, virtually no elevation change.
Land status:	The trail is located on U.S. Army Corps of Engineers property, in the Keg Creek Wildlife Management Area. This is a multi-use trail; please respect the rights of other users.
Maps:	USGS Leah.
Access:	From Atlanta, go east on Interstate 20 to Exit 60 for Georgia Highway 150. Go left 10.5 miles on GA 150 to Pollard's Corner, at the intersection of GA 150/47 and GA 104/221. Make a sharp left on GA 47 and go 1.6 miles. You will see a gated roadbed and a sign for the Keg Creek WMA to your left. Continue on GA 47 for another 0.4 mile until you see a small dirt parking area and trailhead to your left. The ride starts from this parking area. If you cross the bridge over the lake, you've gone too far.

Notes on the trail: Just a few miles from Mistletoe State Park, the Keg Creek Loop winds around part of the shore of Clarks Hill Lake, through sighing pine forests, older hardwood stands, and across several feeder creeks along the way. You'll notice that this ride has no elevation graph with it. That's because the entire ride is flat and hovers around 350 feet above sea level, except for one little hop to 415 feet.

Does this mean Keg Creek's too easy a ride? Nope. Every ride teaches you something; Keg Creek will teach you how to ride over logs and cross drainage dips—dozens of them. But this is not a bad thing. The logs are all a rideable size, and the dips are almost all rideable (you can guess which ones aren't). By the time you've finished this ride, you'll be a much better log-hopper and dip-dasher, and the trail, with or without the obstacles, is some of the sweetest pine-carpeted singletrack I've ridden in Georgia. After a weekend here you'll be ready for steeper and more technical challenges.

Keg Creek Loop

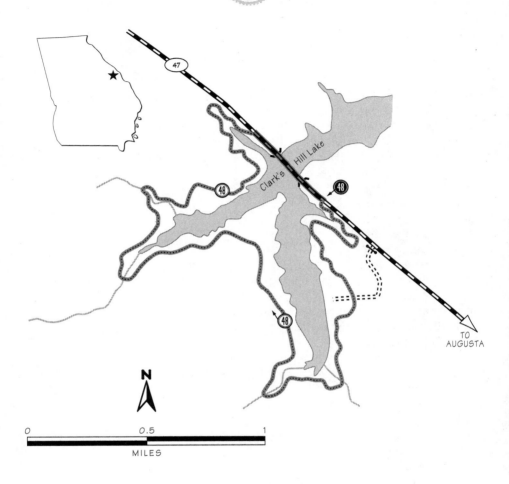

Clark's Hill Lake

47

48

48

48

TO AUGUSTA

N

0   0.5   1

MILES

Restrictions: This trail is located within a wildlife management area, and the trails are closed during scheduled hunting days. Please check the bulletin board at the trailhead, or call the number listed in Appendix C for information.

THE RIDE

0.0 The trail enters the woods at the parking area. The trail is marked with yellow blazes. The trail enters the woods and crosses a small stream.

0.1 Cross a footbridge.

0.2 Cross another footbridge.

0.4 Cross a footbridge; you'll join the lakeshore, then cross another footbridge.

0.5 Wildlife opening to the left.

0.6 Creek crossing.

1.1 Stream crossing.

1.3 Creek crossing.

1.4 Stream crossing.

1.7 Creek crossing.

1.75 Cross a footbridge and turn right.

2.5 Trail turns sharp left by a large pine tree; look for yellow blazes to the left.

2.6 Stream crossing.

3.1 Trail intersects with a woods road; go straight across.

3.5 Trail turns sharp right off an old roadbed.

3.6 Cross a footbridge.

4.0 Stream crossing.

4.1 Stream crossing followed shortly by a creek crossing.

4.5 Stream crossing.

4.7 Creek crossing.

5.5 Creek crossing.

5.6 Huge tree beside the trail.

6.2 Creek crossing.

6.4 Cross a footbridge.

6.5 Trail forks; go right along the lakeshore.

6.8 Trail intersects with another trail; go straight and cross a footbridge.

7.0 Cross a footbridge.

7.2 Cross a series of footbridges and a stream.

7.3 Trail forks; go left and follow the yellow blazes.

7.4 Trail ends at a parking lot beside GA 47. Go right and ride across the bridge, along the paved road for 0.5 mile. (Caution: There is no bike lane on GA 47.)

7.9 Ride ends at the trailhead.

More Rides

49

Road and Trail Cyclery

Location:	Near Oxford, about 30 minutes east of Atlanta.
Distance:	5.8 miles.
Time:	1.25 hours.
Tread:	5.8 miles on singletrack and doubletrack, some on old roadbeds.
Aerobic level:	Moderate.
Technical difficulty:	3.
Highlights:	Tight, twisty singletrack, double dips and gullies, wildlife, and a bike wash and on-site bike shop.
Land status:	The trail is located entirely on private property.
Maps:	USGS Milstead.
Access:	From Atlanta, go east on Interstate 20 to Exit 46 for Georgia Highway 142. Turn left and go 2.7 miles to Airport Road on the right. Turn right and go 0.4 mile to the Road and Trail Cyclery on the right. Park in the lot in front of the bike shop. You must sign a release form at the shop to ride here.

Notes on the trail: This trail is another example of the positive results when an enthusiast is also a landowner. This trail has a little of everything, from a short slickrock section, to a twist-fest with multiple single, double, and triple dips through the piny woods to a couple of deceptively tricky stream crossings. There are footbridges over the more difficult water crossings. One section runs along a cleared powerline cut, and the quasi-quicksand water crossing at the bottom is a great launching pad into the opposite bank (personal experience again). Though the trail has no extended climbs, a couple of short steep ones will get your attention. The trail loops back on or crosses itself a couple of times, but is usually well marked with ribbon and easy to follow. This trail is used as a race course several times a year. It presents a deceptively challenging stop on the state points series, and is one of the favorites with Georgia racers. Owner Al Strickland has been a staunch supporter of mountain bike racing; the presence of a full-service bike shop and BMX track at the site is an example of Al's commitment to the sport for

Road and Trail Cyclery

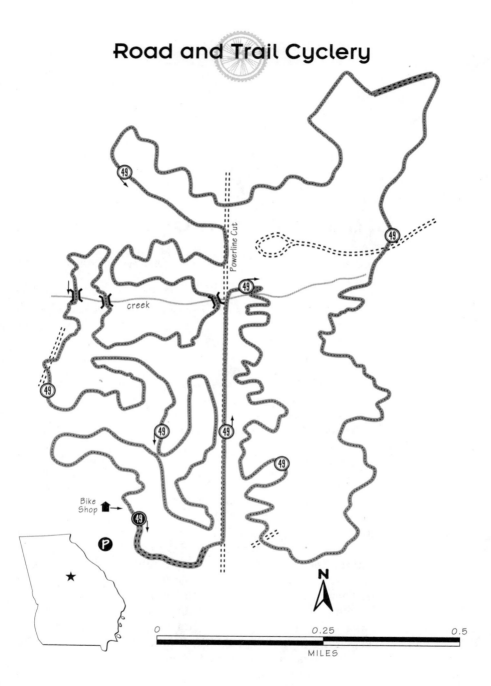

Powerline Cut

creek

49

Bike Shop

P

N

0   0.25   0.5

MILES

Windridge Farm area.

all levels and ages. Whether you come to race or ride, you'll be challenged here.

Restrictions: This trail is closed to casual riding during races. You must sign a release form before you ride the trail. Call 770-787-8193 for schedules and fee information. Please respect the rights of the owners.

THE RIDE

49. Road and Trail Cyclery

- **0.0** From the parking lot, the trail leaves to the right if you're facing the shop. It turns left and follows an old roadbed, past an abandoned mobile home.
- **0.2** Trail enters the powerline cut and turns left.
- **0.4** Water crossing. (Watch for quasi-quicksand here!) Just across the water, turn right and re-enter the woods.
- **0.5** Turn right across a footbridge, then turn left.
- **0.7** Mini-slickrock section.
- **1.5** Stream crossing.
- **1.9** Enter a clearing cross over a culvert, then turn left back into the woods.
- **2.1** At the clearing turn right onto an old roadbed.
- **2.2** Roadbed forks; go right.

2.4	Trail turns sharp left off the roadbed.
2.5	Stream crossing. Just beyond this, turn left onto a roadbed, then turn sharp right and cross a creek. The trail is following an old roadbed.
2.6	Enter a clearcut; the roadbed goes right and the trail goes straight along the clearcut and rejoins another roadbed farther along the clearing.
2.9	Roadbed enters from the right; the trail turns left.
3.0	Trail crosses a powerline cut and re-enters the woods.
3.4	Trail briefly joins the powerline cut, then re-enters the woods.
3.7	Stream crossing.
3.9	Trail turns right and crosses a footbridge next to the powerline cut. Turn right after you cross the footbridge.
4.0	Stream crossing.
4.2	Halfway up a short steep uphill, the trail forks; go right. Just ahead is another fork; go right.
4.3	Cross a footbridge.
4.4	Cross a footbridge.
4.5	Trail leaves to the right; go straight along the hillside.
4.8	Trail enters from the right; stay straight.
4.9	Trail briefly joins an old roadbed, then forks left off the roadbed.
5.3	Just past an old shed, the trail forks; go right.
5.4	Trail rejoins an old roadbed that intersects with another roadbed; go left up the technical climb.
5.5	Trail enters a clearing; go right.
5.6	Trail passes the BMX track; stay left.
5.7	Trail goes down an old rutted roadbed, then climbs back into a clearing behind the scoring shed.
5.8	Ride ends at the parking lot.

Windridge Farm

Location:	8 miles west of Newnan, about 1 hour from Atlanta.
Distance:	The loop described is 7.6 miles.
Time:	1.25 hours (hammerhead racers can do this trail in under 30 minutes).
Tread:	6.7 miles on singletrack, and 0.9 mile on woods road.
Aerobic level:	Moderate.
Technical difficulty:	3.5.
Highlights:	A variety of wildlife, tight, twisty singletrack, a mini-slickrock section, refreshing lake.

Windridge Farm

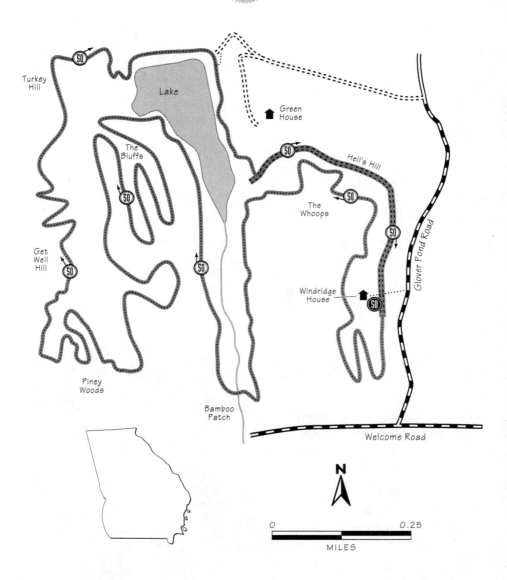

Turkey Hill

Lake

Green House

The Bluffs

Hell's Hill

The Whoops

Get Well Hill

Windridge House

Glover Pond Road

Piney Woods

Bamboo Patch

Welcome Road

N

0   0.25

MILES

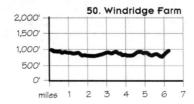

50. Windridge Farm

2,000'
1,500'
1,000'
500'
0'

miles   1   2   3   4   5   6   7

Land status:	Windridge Farm is located on private property. There is a fee to ride. For information, call 770-253-6510.
Maps:	USGS Franklin and Newnan Southwest.
Access:	From Atlanta, follow Interstate 85 south to Exit 9. Go right 0.6 mile to the second traffic light. Turn right on the Georgia Highway 34 bypass. Follow this road through several intersections, approximately 5.5 miles to Welcome Road, on your left. Turn left here, and again at the stop sign by the bridge. Follow Welcome Road about 9.5 miles through two four-way stops and a name change. Turn right onto Glover Pond Road and go about 0.8 mile, then turn left into a concrete driveway and park in the designated area. You must sign in at the house before riding.

Notes on the trail: Windridge Farm is a good example of the possibilities when property owners are also enthusiasts. Owners Steven and Jennie Sellen have created an interesting option to the typical public trail. Situated on just over 200 acres of a Civil War–era farm, the trail layout makes great use of the terrain. The trail is almost entirely singletrack, with a few woods road-beds thrown in for confusion. The downhills are technical and challenging, and the climbs are moderate but short. There are drop-offs over old terraces, several rock gardens, and all sorts of other goodies; your technical skills will get a workout here. Windridge Farm is used as a race course several times a year, and is a favorite among local racers.

Beautiful singletrack along a lake in the Windridge Farm area.

There are also several mini-ecosystems within the ride, from a windswept piece of slickrock with an overlook of the surrounding hills, to a piny woods, to a bamboo patch down along the beaver ponds. The lake is hidden on the lower part of the ride, and tempts you with its refreshing waters. In the fall, the foliage is especially striking when reflecting off the lake's surface. The trail itself has enough variety and challenges to keep your undivided attention the first few laps, but take some time to enjoy the surroundings. The trail shows some personal touches, with descriptive section names such as The Bluffs, Piney Woods, and Hell's Hill.

Restrictions: Windridge Farm is private property that is open to all riders on weekends, and members during the week. You must pay a fee (currently $3 per rider per day, or annual memberships are available), and you must sign in at the house. Trespassers will be prosecuted! It is always recommended that you call the day before you visit because various events will sometimes close the trail to casual riding.

THE RIDE

0.0 From the parking area, follow the old roadbed up the hill.

0.1 Trail enters the woods, singletrack begins.

0.5 Trail intersection; go left.

0.7 Trail intersects an old roadbed; go left, then immediately right back onto the singletrack.

1.0 Trail intersects an old roadbed; go left, then immediately right back onto the singletrack.

1.4 Trail enters from the right, go straight.

1.7 Trail enters from the right; go straight.

2.0 Creek crossing; enter a bamboo patch.

2.2 Cross an old roadbed.

2.5 Trail enters from the right; go straight.

3.7 Cross an old roadbed.

4.0 Trail enters a roadbed; go right.

4.1 Trail forks; go right.

5.4 Trail intersects a roadbed; go left, then immediately right back onto the singletrack.

5.9 Cross an old roadbed.

6.6 Trail intersection; go left.

6.7 Trail crosses a dam; go right on singletrack after you cross the dam.

7.1 Trail enters a roadbed; go left up the hill.

7.2 Trail enters an open field; go past the greenhouse on the roadbed back into the woods.

7.6 Trail ends at the parking area.

Other Rides

Two and a half years ago, when I did the initial research for this project, I was confident that I had included the bulk of the good bike trails in the state. Almost all of these trails are in the mountainous northern part of Georgia. Although this guide includes the majority of the state's trails, the sweeping changes in the past two years have created a frustrating situation for me. With the Georgia Department of Natural Resources and other federal and state land management agencies realizing the recreational value of bike trails, and the resulting creation or conversion of many of the state park's trail systems to bike or multi-use, I had to include a much larger "Other Rides" section than I would have liked.

- Countless combinations of gravel county and Forest Service roads lace the Chattahoochee-Oconee National Forest. Get a map and explore for yourself. Just remember that although the gravel roads are open to bikes, trails are not unless signed specifically for bikes. The Appalachian Trail is absolutely not open to bikes under any circumstances. Also remember to take some precautions and pack extra gear for undetermined length rides.

- The first ever Olympic Mountain Bike race course is located in Conyers, just east of Atlanta. While the course is open to the public on a fee basis, major changes and reroutes planned for the site make an in-depth ride description immediately obsolete and inaccurate, so I have not included it in this guide.

- The Bull Mountain/Jake Mountain area has approximately 28 more miles of multi-use trails in the existing plans for the next 2 years.

- Additional trails are planned at Chicopee Woods, as well as a connecting bike route from Gainesville College to the trails.

- Bike and equestrian trails are planned for the new Chattahoochee State Park, just south of Gainesville. The completion date is unknown because such projects are always subject to funding snafus.

- Construction is under way on a 5- to 7-mile multi-use loop at Fort Yargo State Park, just northeast of Atlanta.

- Plans have been under discussion for the past few years for a linear park in Woodstock, just north of Atlanta, that would include several miles of multi-use trails.

- Gwinnett County, in metro Atlanta, owns a piece of property along the Yellow River just behind Stone Mountain that already has bike trails on it. The property is now part of the County Parks and Recreation Department, which will maintain the trail system.

172

- The Simms Mountain Trail, about 5 miles long, will open near Rome soon.

- Magnolia Springs State Park has opened a 5- to 7-mile loop to mountain bikes.

- Stephen C. Foster State Park has access to national forestlands laced with forest roads that can be ridden.

- Alexander Stephens State Park has a 5-mile network of easy to moderate hiking and cycling trails.

- Victoria Bryant State Park has a 5-mile loop that is popular with local cyclists.

- Just outside Amicalola Falls State Park is a large area of national forest laced with roads and trails. A local favorite ride leaves from here, but is not properly marked, and even returning riders tend to get "misplaced" here occasionally.

- The trail in the National Park Service's Chattahoochee River National Recreation Area along Sope Creek is still open to bikes, but the amount of users and the limited trail area makes me reluctant to include it here.

- The Cumberland Island National Seashore, just off the Georgia coast, has about 50 miles of dirt and sand roads that are available for mountain biking.

- There are several privately owned properties that host races and events several times a year, but are not open to the general riding public most of the time. You can contact the Georgia Association of Promoters for more information. Rides on private property don't usually get included unless there's a long history of the property owners having the trail open, and the property is not in an area that will almost certainly see development.

Glossary

ATB: All-terrain bicycle; a.k.a., mountain bike, sprocket rocket, fat tire flyer.

ATV: All-terrain vehicle; in this book ATV refers to motorbikes and three- and four-wheelers designed for off-road use.

Bail: Getting off the bike, usually in a hurry, whether or not you meant to. Often a last resort.

Bunny hop: Leaping up, while riding, and lifting both wheels off the ground to jump over an obstacle (or for sheer joy).

Clamper cramps: That burning, cramping sensation experienced in the hands during extended braking.

Clean: To ride without touching a foot (or other body part) to the ground; to ride a tough section successfully.

Clipless: A type of pedal with a binding that accepts a special cleat on the soles of bike shoes. The cleat clicks in for more control and efficient pedaling and out for safe landings (in theory).

Contour: A line on a topographic map showing a continuous elevation level over uneven ground. Also used as a verb to indicate a fairly easy or moderate grade: "The trail contours around the canyon rim before the final grunt to the top."

Dab: To put a foot or hand down (or hold on to or lean on a tree or other support) while riding. If you have to dab, then you haven't ridden that piece of trail *clean*.

Downfall: Trees that have fallen across the trail.

Doubletrack: A trail, jeep road, ATV route, or other track with two distinct ribbons of *tread*, typically with grass growing in between. No matter which side you choose, the other rut always looks smoother.

Endo: Lifting the rear wheel off the ground and riding (or abruptly not riding) on the front wheel only. Also known, at various degrees of control and finality, as a nose wheelie, going over the handlebars, and a face plant.

Fall line: The angle and direction of a slope; the *line* you follow when gravity is in control and you aren't.

Graded: When a gravel road is scraped level to smooth out the washboards and potholes, it has been graded. In this book, a road is listed as graded only if it is regularly maintained. Not all such roads are graded every year, however.

Granny gear: The lowest (easiest) gear, a combination of the smallest of the three chain rings on the bottom bracket spindle (where the pedals and crank arms attach to the bike's frame) and the largest cog on the rear cluster. Shift down to your granny gear for serious climbing.

Hammer: To ride hard; derived from how it feels afterward: "I'm hammered."

Hammerhead: Someone who actually enjoys feeling *hammered*. A type-A personality rider who goes hard and fast all the time.

Kelly hump: An abrupt mound of dirt across the road or trail. These are common on old logging roads and skidder tracks, placed there to block vehicle access. At high speeds, they become launching pads for bikes and inadvertent astronauts.

Line: The route (or trajectory) between or over obstacles or through turns. *Tread* or trail refers to the ground you're riding on; the line is the path you choose within the tread (and exists mostly in the eye of the beholder).

Off-the-seat: Moving your butt behind the bike seat and over the rear tire; used for control on extremely steep descents. This position increases braking power, helps prevent *endos*, and reduces skidding.

Portage: To carry the bike, usually up a steep hill, across unrideable obstacles, or through a stream.

Quads: Thigh muscles (short for quadriceps) or maps in the USGS topographic series (short for quadrangles). Nice quads of either kind can help get you out of trouble in the backcountry.

Ratcheting: Also known as backpedaling; pedaling backward to avoid hitting rocks or other obstacles with the pedals.

Sidehill: Where the trail crosses a slope. If the *tread* is narrow, keep your inside (uphill) pedal up to avoid hitting the ground. If the tread tilts downhill, you may have to use some body language to keep the bike plumb or vertical to avoid slipping out.

Singletrack: A trail, game run, or other track with only one ribbon of *tread*. But this is like defining an orgasm as a muscle cramp. Good singletrack is pure fun.

Spur: A side road or trail that splits off from the main route.

Surf: Riding through loose gravel or sand, when the wheels sway from side to side. Also heavy surf: frequent and difficult obstacles.

Suspension: A bike with front suspension has a shock-absorbing fork or stem. Rear suspension absorbs shock between the rear wheel and frame. A bike with both is said to be fully suspended.

Switchbacks: When a trail goes up a steep slope, it zigzags or *switchbacks* across the *fall line* to ease the gradient of the climb. Well-designed switchbacks make a turn with at least an 8-foot radius and remain fairly level within the turn itself. These are rare, however, and cyclists often struggle to ride through sharply angled, sloping switchbacks.

Track stand: Balancing on a bike in one place, without rolling forward appreciably. Cock the front wheel to one side and bring that pedal up to the one or two o'clock position. Now control your side-to-side balance by applying pressure on the pedals and brakes and changing the angle of the front wheel, as needed. It takes practice but really comes in handy at stoplights, on *switchbacks*, and when trying to free a foot before falling.

Tread: The riding surface, particularly regarding *singletrack*.

Water bar: A log, rock, or other barrier placed in the *tread* to divert water off the trail and prevent erosion. Peeled logs can be slippery and cause bad falls, especially when they angle sharply across the trail.

Whoop-dee-doo: A series of kelly humps used to keep vehicles off trails. Watch your speed or do the dreaded top tube tango.

Appendix A: Volunteering

I've often looked around me at a work party and wondered at seeing some of the same people almost every week coming out to spend a day helping build trails. It's almost as if we actually enjoy the work as much as the riding. To say that seems ludicrous, yet more than a few of us probably work more than we ride. Why?

I can only answer for myself: I think most people want to leave something behind. I'm no exception. Trail building is such an anonymous art. Seldom will you ever see the names of the people who helped build and maintain a trail published anywhere. Where would you print it? Who would read it? We deal with such a remote and detached part of everyday life that few people ever come out to see what we've done, and far fewer realize that most of the work was done by volunteers.

I got to name Bare Hare Trail, because I was there with Tony Rider, the Forest Service ranger, when we found a tuft of bear fur on a tree next to the trail on one of our work parties. Tony liked the idea and the name stuck. (Jay Franklin created the alternate spelling because there was already a Bear Hair Trail in North Georgia.) It doesn't mean much to anyone but me, but if my grandchildren enjoy the same great experience I have when I ride that trail, then I've helped to leave them something worthwhile. The naming story can be a part of family lore. Of course, having a trail named after you would be great, but I think you have to die on it or something for that to happen.

Anyway, next time you have a good ride or hike on a great trail, remember that each trail is the sum of the efforts of many. When you think of it that way, the trail begins to take on a life of its own as a living thing that grows, ages, and changes, and must be nurtured and cared for. And that without such care could just as quickly be gone.

How to Get Involved

If you visit the area, or live here and are just looking for more ride opportunities, take some time to pitch in and do your part to help ensure that the area continues to experience growth in land access and trail opportunities.

There are many ways to get involved. Swinging a pulaski or fire rake, or running a chainsaw are not the only ways to help. Though some of us actually like the hard work and camaraderie that work parties bring, we do understand that others might not get the same kick out of building something. Other tasks include marketing, adminstration, and fundraising.

The Southern Off-Road Bicycle Association (SORBA) was incorporated in the state of Georgia in 1989 by a small group of dedicated volunteers facing a trail closure. SORBA members have worked hard over the years to establish the group as one of the more successful land access and advocacy organizations in the country. As I traveled the state for this book, I was constantly amazed by the far-reaching effects of the efforts of the volunteers.

Contrary to local beliefs, SORBA members actually do ride their bikes quite often. Organized rides are a large part of the club's activities.

SORBA Membership Application

Individual $15.00

Family $20.00

Organization $25.00

SORBA & IMBA $25.00*

Renewal

Change of Address

Land Access Donation $____
(donations are tax deductible)

Last Name: _____

First Name: _____

Address: _____

City: _____ State: _____

Zip: _____ Age: _____

Phone (H) _____

Phone (W) _____

E-mail: _____

Other Club Affiliations:_____

Chapter:

    Athens

    Atlanta

    Ellijay

    Gainesville

    Helen

    Northeast Georgia

I am interested in helping with:

Trail Maintenance

Telephone Committee

Fat Tire Times Production

Fat Tire Times Distribution

Festival Committee

Race Volunteer

Ride Leader

In consideration of my membership, I agree to not hold the Southern Off-Road Bicycle Association, Inc. (SORBA), or any of its members liable for any injury or damage, however caused, which may result from participation in any event sponsored by SORBA.

Signature: _____

Parent or Guardian if Under18: _____

*Combination for individuals only

Mail to : SORBA
       P.O. Box 671774
       Marietta, GA 30006

Appendix B: Land Access Organizations

Mecca Trails Association
706-832-8496 (Augusta area)

Southern Off-Road Bicycling Association
(SORBA)
P.O. Box 671774
Marietta, GA 30006
770-565-1795
www.sorba.org

SORBA-Athens Chapter
www.sorba.org

SORBA-Gainesville Chapter
770-534-1279

Ellijay Mountain Bike Association
706-635-2453

SORBA-Helen Chapter
706-878-3715

SORBA-Northeast Georgia Chapter
706-782-2407

International Mountain Bicycling Association (IMBA)
P.O. Box 7578
Boulder CO, 80306
303-545-9011
www.imba.com

Georgia Association of Promoters (GAP)
P.O. Box 675167
Marietta, GA 30006-0011

Appendix C: Land Management Agencies

Chattahoochee-Oconee
National Forest

Forest Supervisor's Office
1755 Cleveland Highway
Gainesville, GA 30501
770-536-0141

Armuchee Ranger District
806 East Villanow Street
LaFayette, GA 30728
706-638-1085

Brasstown Ranger District
P.O. Box 9
Blairsville, GA 30512
706-745-6928

Chattooga Ranger District
200 Highway 197 North
Clarkesville, GA 30523
706-754-6221

Cohutta Ranger District
401 GI Maddox Parkway
Chatsworth, GA 30705
706-695-6736

Tallulah Ranger District
809 Highway 441 South
Clayton, GA 30525
706-782-3320

Toccoa Ranger District
6050 Appalachian Parkway
Blue Ridge, GA 30513
706-632-3031

U.S. Army Corps of Engineers

Carters Lake Project Management Office
P.O. Box 96
Oakman, GA 30732
706-334-2248

J. Strom Thurmond Project Office
Route 1, Box 12
Clarks Hill, SC 29821
864-333-1100

Georgia Department of Natural
Resources
Wildlife Resources Division
Game Management Section (for hunting
schedules on wildlife management areas)
770-918-6404
www.DNR.State.GA.US

Georgia State Parks
www.serve.com/bike/georgia/trails

Central Reservations Office (for camping and cottage rentals)
1-800-864-7275
770-389-7275
TDD 770-389-7404

Amicalola Falls State Park and Lodge
418 Amicalola Falls Lodge Road
Dawsonville, GA 30534
706-265-8888

Fort Mountain State Park
181 Fort Mountain Park Road
Chatsworth, GA 30705
706-695-2621

Fort Yargo State Park
P.O. Box 764
Winder, GA 30680
706-867-3489

Magnolia Springs State Park
Route 5, Box 488
Millen, GA 30442
912-982-1660

Mistletoe State Park
3723 Mistletoe Road
Appling, GA 30802
706-541-0321

Stephen C. Foster State Park
Route 1, Box 131
Fargo, GA 31631
912-637-5274

Tallulah Gorge State Park
P.O. Box 248
Tallulah Falls, GA 30573
706-754-7970

Unicoi State Park and Lodge
P.O. Box 849
Helen, GA 30545
706-878-2201

Victoria Bryant State Park
1105 Bryant Park Road
Royston, GA 30662
706-245-6270

Private Property Operators

Road & Trail Cyclery
1569 Airport Road
Oxford, GA 30054
770-787-8193
(trail, race courses, and full-service bike shop)

Windridge Farm
420 Glover Pond Road
Newnan, GA 30263
770-253-6510
(trail and race course)

Appendix D: Bike Shops

The following shops are closest to the trails.

Adventure Cycles
4619 Smithson Boulevard
Oakwood, GA 30566
770-534-1190
(full-service bike shop)

Biketown USA
1604 Dawsonville Highway
Gainesville, GA 30501
770-532-7090
(full-service bike shop)

Bob's Cycle Shop
2203 Shorter Avenue
Rome, GA 30165
706-291-1501
(full-service bike shop)

Cartecay River Bicycles
4027 Highway 52 East
Ellijay, GA 30540
706-635-2453
888-276-2453
(tours and full-service bike shop)

Chain Reaction Cycle & Fitness
3920 Roberts Road
Martinez (Augusta), GA 30907
706-855-2024
(full-service bike shop)

Dalton Bicycle Works
1107 East Walnut
Dalton, GA 30721
706-279-2558
(full-service bike shop)

Mountaintown Outdoor Expeditions
P.O. Box 86
Ellijay, GA 30540
706-635-2524
(tours and races)

Mountain Adventures Cyclery
251 A Highway 400
Dahlonega, GA 30533
706-864-8525
(tours and full-service bike shop)

Outspokin
592 Bobby Jones Expressway Suite 20
Augusta, GA 30907
706-868-6788
(full-service bike shop)

Woody's Mountain Bikes
P.O. Box 774
Helen, GA 30545
706-878-3715
(tours and full-service bike shop)

North Georgia Bicycle Dealers Association
www.bike4fun.com

Appendix E: Tourist Information

Augusta Metropolitan Convention &
Visitors Bureau
32 Eighth Street
Augusta, GA 30903
706-823-6600

Blue Ridge–Fannin County Chamber of
Commerce
P.O. Box 875
Blue Ridge, GA 30513
800-899-6867

Chatsworth–Murray County Chamber
of Commerce
126 North Third Avenue
Chatsworth, GA 30705
706-695-6060

Dahlonega–Lumpkin County Chamber
of Commerce
13 South Park Street, Dept. G
Dahlonega, GA 30533
706-864-3711
www.dahlonega.org

Gainesville–Hall Convention & Visitors
Bureau
830 Green Street
Gainesville, GA 30501
770-536-5209

Gilmer County Chamber of Commerce
P.O. Box 505, Dept. NE
Ellijay, GA 30540
706-635-7400
www.chamber@ellijay.com

Helen/White County Convention & Visitors Bureau
P.O. Box 730
Helen, GA 30545
800-858-8027

Lake Russell Recreation Area
Dicks Hill Parkway
Mt. Airy, GA 30563
706-754-6221

Rabun County Convention & Visitors
Bureau
P.O. Box 761
Clayton, GA 30525
706-782-4812

Georgia Department of Industry, Trade,
& Tourism
P.O. Box 1776
Atlanta, GA 30301
404-656-3590

Index

Page numbers in *italics* refer to photos.
Page numbers in **bold** refer to maps.